Real Market Economics

Philip Rush

Real Market Economics

The Fundamental Framework for Finance Practitioners

palgrave
macmillan

Philip Rush
Heteronomics
City of London, UK

ISBN 978-1-349-95277-9 ISBN 978-1-349-95278-6 (eBook)
https://doi.org/10.1057/978-1-349-95278-6

Library of Congress Control Number: 2017958969

Cover image: © jacquesdurocher/Getty Images
Cover design by Samantha Johnson

Printed on acid-free paper

This Palgrave Macmillan imprint is published by Springer Nature
The registered company is Macmillan Publishers Ltd.
The registered company address is: The Campus, 4 Crinan Street, London, N1 9XW, United Kingdom

Preface

Economics is about the allocation of resources, so it as at the heart of markets. And yet to many, economics is a field that feels far removed from the realities of what they see trading. Common sense, some entrepreneurial intuition and a decent dose of luck might seem like the only tools one needs to navigate a profitable path, especially when approaching a new financial market. However, this would be a weak framework. It is one where inconsistencies can thrive, cancelling out the rewards of erstwhile successful views or leaving no protection when risks crystallise. Of course, luck is always welcome, but there is no accounting for it. Relying on that for returns is to make those returns ultimately un-replicable and thus unstable—a recipe for an unintentionally short relationship with real markets. A robust framework is needed instead, which this book provides.

Unfortunately, there is a chasm between most economic research and what is fundamentally driving real markets. At the academic end, economists insist on talking to themselves and pursuing niche research over addressing the needs of those allocating resources. It is almost another language, so it should not be surprising when people struggle to realise the relevance of economics. City economists bridge some of the gaps, but only for select clients. The business relies on dependence to justify hefty fees. It is like fishers fetching a higher price from those who cannot catch fish themselves. Those who lack understanding in our product or the willingness to pay will also find many in this smelly business passing goldfish off as an excellent tuna steak. Most people must make do with superficial portions. Readers of this book should learn to tell the difference and how to start catching metaphorical fish for themselves.

This book's originality is mainly its existence, rather than most of the ideas within it. Numerous other books address select issues of relevance to real markets, but they are narrow and deep. Reading them will not provide the robust framework needed. Meanwhile, the general and lengthy books from academia might have tremendous breadth, but even "applied" ones are poorly suited to practitioners, who are not the target audience. If you want a book that will abstractly teach you mainstream economic thought and its workhorse model as gospel, there are lots of books of that ilk. Mastering their mainstream models will open up many well-paid jobs re-teaching the same skills or applying them for places not subject to normal market pressures, i.e. government payrolls in all their guises, including central banks. However, if you want to make serious money instead, you need to be where the profits are. That means participating in real markets where many conventional assumptions are simply wrong. Properly placed, the realism of models that relax such assumptions brings their rewards. And a working knowledge can be attained relatively quickly.

Before we can start massaging out theoretical tensions, we need to make sure the framework is forming on strong foundations. It cannot be robust without that. Challenges to even the basic economic concepts will nonetheless be tackled here as promptly as it is possible to do so without causing unnecessary confusion. Correcting the theoretical foundations after they've set is an unnecessarily difficult task that also leaves inappropriate foundations in the interim. The first part of this book builds up the core framework of economic concepts, starting with real levels of activity before turning to growth in it and then prices, amid the dynamics of business cycles. Part two adds on the stabilising crossbeams, including macroprudential policies next to the more conventional monetary and fiscal ones. It naturally addresses how we might watch and anticipate changes in these policies. Finally, part three liberally coats the framework with financial markets, thereby making the completed framework's robust structure useful for investing in real markets.

City of London, UK Philip Rush

Contents

List of Figures

Part I

The Economy

It would be an odd economics book indeed that didn't cover the core economic concepts. The applicability of this one to real markets does not make it an exception. Indeed, we must know what we are applying before it can be applied! That is not to say a laboured treatment of each concept lies ahead. By choosing a book about economics and markets, you have identified yourself as someone smart, even if you've never decided to study such things before. So I shall not insult you by pretending you need transferable concepts reintroduced from scratch each time. Nor will I provide repetitive derivations and "proofs" here, especially as the latter are rarely of useful things. Much better to move quickly enough that the linkages between concepts flow. This book's unrepentant focus will be on what you need to know to form a robust framework that is genuinely applicable to real markets. As the useful stuff includes the exceptions that arise outside dodgy assumptions, some of it might come as a surprise even to students of economics.

The foundations for our framework are in the fundamental truths of human action. It is by the self-interested actions of individuals that effective demands and production follows. Monitoring this is a problem that forces us to rely on aggregate data, despite the dangers of doing so, which are ignored all too frequently. We will review the relevance and interrelationships of the national accounts data here. As real growth ultimately just boils down to productivity and labour supply, we will focus on those concepts and some of the associated forecasting basics. As is often optimal and logical, we do this in volume terms first. Growth in the value of expenditure associated with rising prices is usually of less relevance. Nonetheless, as prices do not change uniformly, there will be relative winners and losers from price movements. The cause of them is crucial, with one-off shocks, shifts in inflation expectations and cyclical capacity pressures carrying different conclusions. Despite the centrality of the latter to this and many other core economic questions, mainstream models represent the nature of the business cycle poorly. Fortunately, the adoption of more realistic assumptions opens up explanations. Having to deal with complex dynamics is the price we pay for this, and yet that is also the point because complexity is at the heart of real markets.

1
Foundations

At its heart, economics is about human action. It is the rational self-interest of individuals that ultimately determines the allocation of resources. Rationality is not to say that people always make the right decision or even that they seek to maximise profits. People are fallible and crave things other than profit, so charitable behaviour can still be rational even if it is not necessarily financially optimal. This perspective may challenge some fundamental theories, but it is not an insurmountable problem. It is warts and all outcomes of individual decisions that determine what the economy does. Complexity abounds as a result, but that is the beauty of it all.

Large corporations are sometimes branded as better matching the modern economic structure. This perspective has some truth from the production perspective nowadays, but there are still fallible individuals at the helm with foibles that are crucial to understanding corporate behaviours. Companies of all sizes are in any case aiming to fulfil the demands of their individual consumers profitably. If the next generation iPhone were just an old Nokia 3210, even devout fans of the brand would desert the company for a competitor. No amount of marketing would change that, contrary to the apparent view of some anti-capitalists who see people as pathetically gullible.

This chapter starts from this grounding of economics in human actions and formalises a framework for how we might determine effective demands. This approach treats people as trying to maximise the personal value they can get from their money. Or put in more mathematical terms, that means maximising utility subject to a budget constraint. Once the demand decision and some quirky cases are cleared up, there will be an exploration of the production side of the economy. Knowing the theoretical basics of how

P. Rush, *Real Market Economics*,
https://doi.org/10.1057/978-1-349-95278-6_1

companies set prices and stay solvent can be invaluable for understanding how real markets will move. Addressing some market imperfections will provide an additional level of useful depth. Finally, this chapter will cover how the aggregate level of activity is measured and how balance sheet positions accumulate as a result of it.

1.1 Demand

No one wants for nothing. In fact, we might describe humanity more reasonably as having unlimited wants and limited resources. Economics is ultimately about the allocation of those resources. Microeconomists naturally spend a lot of time debating how those demands lead to trade-offs. At a more macrolevel, though, these observed behaviours influence how businesses seek to set their prices and anticipate how changes in relative prices and incomes might impact their sales by extension.

1.1.1 Indifference Curves

Everyone has their personal intrinsic values and preferences that determine their demands. In its simplest form, we can view this as a trade-off between two things, like having cakes and eating them, as shown by the "indifference curves" in Fig. 1.1. As with most things, there is not a linear relationship here. The value of eating more cakes falls the more you've eaten—you'll start

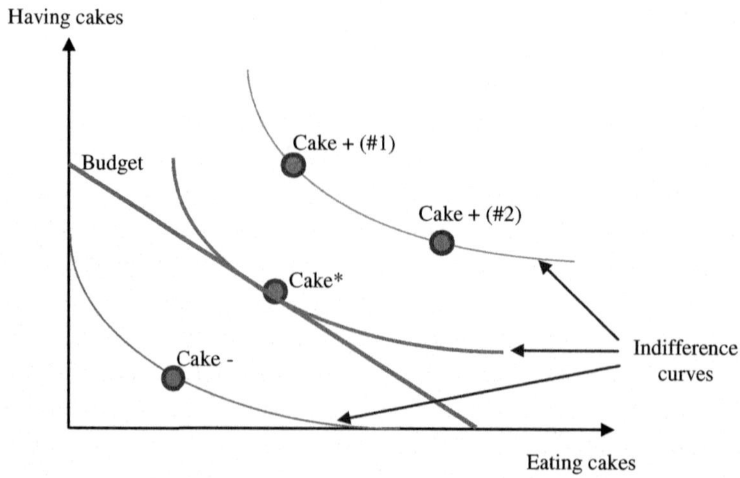

Fig. 1.1 Indifference curves

to get full—with the value of having the cake for later going up instead. Or vice versa, eating cake when you're holding a mountain of them will be more tempting.

For a given set of preferences, someone might be indifferent between points #1 and #2 on the Cake+ line. Either position gives the person far more cake to both have and eat than any point on the Cake- line, so they'd rather have that option if it exists. In general, an economist would say that higher indifference curves are always preferred to lower ones, which is important when we remember that there is always a constraint. The point where the highest indifference curve touches the budget constraint maximises utility (i.e. Cake*). That's the tasty point where you are eating exactly the right proportion of the cakes you have.

The previous example is a theoretical snapshot rather than something to directly observe and exploit. As prices and income changes, preferences can shift this snapshot. What business can do is vary their prices, which effectively pivots the budget constraint line, as shown in the cakes and cookies trade-off of Fig. 1.2. By observing what happens to the demand for cookies as its price changes, a demand curve can be built up. By extension, from changing relative prices, the marginal rate of substation between products can also be estimated. Shifts to online shopping portals are lowering the costs and difficulties of changing prices and running such experiments. And as incomes evolve over time, or as we observe behaviours between different consumer groups, the variation of relative demand to income can also be derived (dubbed an Engel curve when plotted). In most cases, we would

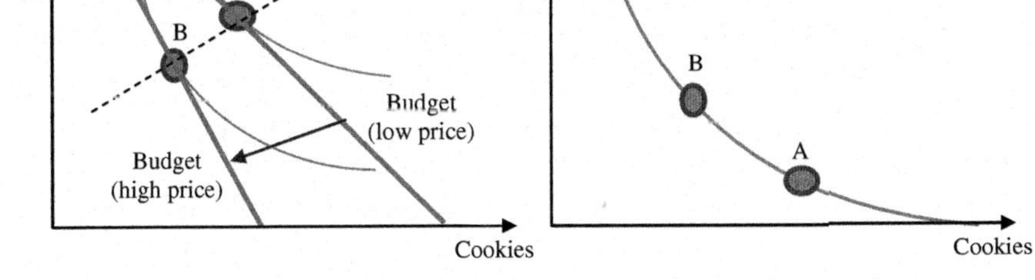

Fig. 1.2 The demand curve

expect higher prices to discourage purchases in favour of something else, while higher incomes would normally raise demand.

1.1.2 The Special Ones

There are some special cases where the usual rules don't apply. A simple example is that of a perfect substitute, where a small difference in price can capture all demand when it becomes more competitive. If the price change doesn't stop it being the cheapest or dearest, then there isn't an effect on demand. With online platforms increasingly making identical listings from multiple indistinguishable third-party sellers, this is not as rare an occurrence as it might sound. Nor is it just a phenomenon for goods since services like hotels are increasingly becoming commoditised through listings on price comparison websites.

Another special class to consider is that of so-called Giffen goods, which face falling demand as their prices fall and vice versa. They are an extreme example of "necessary goods", where demand changes by less than income. In this extreme, though, when the price of something fundamental and unavoidable for survival rises, people end up with less to spend on other things and so have to buy even more of the good, despite its higher price. That may sound implausible in modern developed countries, but was pertinent during the Irish potato famine and remains so for rice in poorer parts of Asia. Meanwhile, the less extreme example of demand rising less than incomes is an everyday occurrence and core to understanding what the retail industry commonly calls non-discretionary consumption.

1.2 Production

Firms need to understand their current and potential customers demands in order to anticipate what to produce profitably. Turning that into a viable production plan is more than just a demand curve, though. Prices and volumes of potential sales need to be weighed against the costs of producing different volumes. Moreover, in a competitive market, various types of costs count differently towards the optimal production strategy over different horizons, so there are some significant differences to explore.

1.2.1 Costs

It is rare for restrictions to limit a company to only one production option. Different inputs from various producers will cost different amounts at different volumes, so there is a task in itself to find what combination minimises costs. This job amounts to a similar problem as the consumer's demand decision. Difficulty in substituting too heavily away from some inputs creates a nonlinear "isoquant" curve covering the resources needed for a given level of production. Meanwhile, the cost of various input combinations is linear, like the budget constraint in the earlier discussion about demand decisions.

A company could use the mixture at point "A" in Fig. 1.3, but it could also use combination "B", which would cost it less. Combination "C" would be cheaper still but isn't a viable way of producing the desired amount. In general, the lowest Isocost line that touches the isoquant is optimal, exactly as the highest indifference curve for a budget constraint was. That no doubt sounds horribly abstract, but if you know your potential suppliers and production processes, it is a point that can be calculated, with costs minimised for a given level of output as a result.

In the previous example, we looked at what combination of inputs delivers a level of production, which is essentially the variable cost of output. Specifically, variable costs are those costs that increase with production. Such

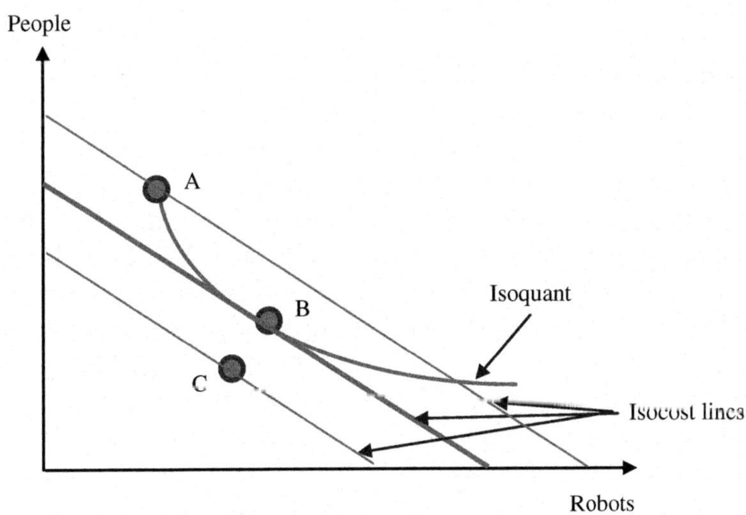

Fig. 1.3 Isocost and isoquant curves

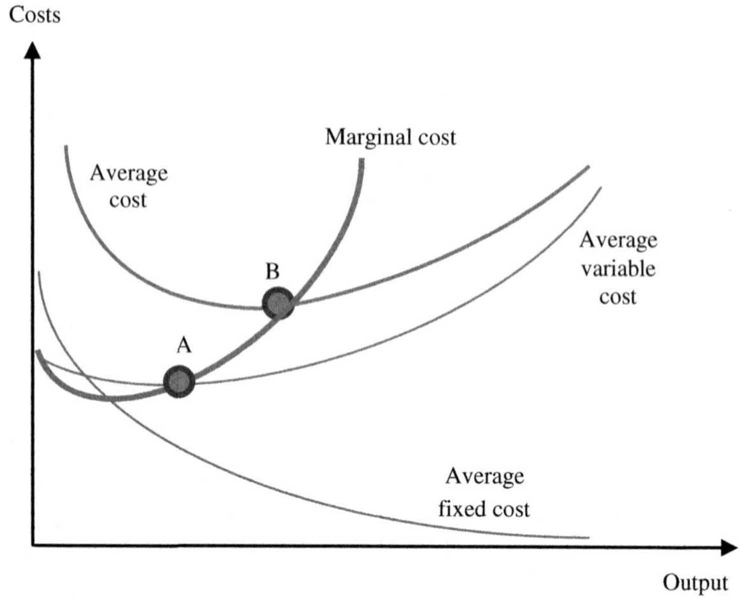

Fig. 1.4 Average and marginal cost curves

costs are related to marginal costs, but whereas the average variable cost is an average of such costs across all output, the marginal cost is only for the production of an additional unit. When a company can enjoy economies of scale—i.e. an additional unit is cheaper than the last—marginal costs are by definition below average variable costs. When inefficiencies dominate, causing diseconomies of scale, the marginal costs will be above instead. That inflexion point is "A" in Fig. 1.4.

There is another class of costs that do not vary with production. They are instead fixed, at least in the short term, and these also influence the optimal level of production. As output increases, fixed costs spread out more, and so the average fixed cost level will fall. A company's actual average costs are a combination of both the average variable and fixed costs. Because of the benefit that comes from spreading fixed costs out further, overall average costs are minimised at a higher level of output than average variable costs (i.e. "B" in Fig. 1.4).

In the long run, companies can vary a variety of short-term fixed things. Contracts might prevent redundancies, changing offices or switching to another supplier. After a change has occurred, the company may be tied in again for some period, and it will face a new short-run average cost curve. As a business would always choose to face the most favourable fixed cost

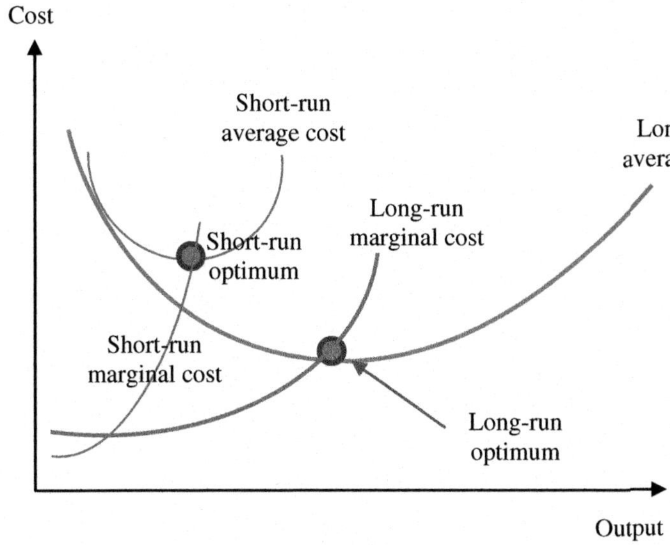

Fig. 1.5 Short-run and long-run cost curves

environment in the long run, we can depict the long-run average cost curve as hugging the bottom of all the potential short-run ones, as in Fig. 1.5. Because of this, the optimum level for minimising average costs will differ between the short run and long run.

1.2.2 Marginals Matter

There is an adage in business that "cost control will keep you whole", but that is only one side of the balance. Companies also need sales. The price achieved in each transaction is the company's marginal revenue on it, and it will be profitable to keep making sales until that marginal revenue is equal to the marginal cost of production. Sell less than that and the company is missing out on some profit, sell more and it is making some of those sales at a loss. For a business in a competitive market where it has little influence on the market price, this means it needs to produce the level of output where its marginal cost of production is equal to the market price. That is where its profits will be maximised, at least in the short run, provided that the price level is above the average variable cost level.

Fixed costs may not matter in the short term, but sales must cover them eventually. If the business isn't profitable enough to do that, it would ultimately be better off shutting down. The sustainable supply curve of a business becomes portions of the marginal cost curve. With the market price above the combined (i.e. fixed + variable) average cost of production, the company can produce at a level that will be profitable in the short run and cover its fixed costs, making it appear sustainable. The resultant supply schedule is illustrated in Fig. 1.6 as the range "A–B" of the marginal cost curve. The dotted range "B–C" does not cover those fixed costs but is profitably covering its variable costs, so supply is possible in this range in the short term.

All of this may seem a bit abstract and theoretical, but it is important to understand this basic framework to anticipate how sustainable prices and businesses are. There is a more applied discussion of this in Chap. 3.1. When moving to real-world applications, we must also remember that what is optimum for a company to produce now does not need to be optimal next year, or in ten years. Some fixed costs are variable over time to the extent that the cost environment could be completely different. Time variability is a crucial but often forgotten fact, especially when we zoom out to more macrolevels where an equilibrium is commonly considered to be a spuriously stable state.

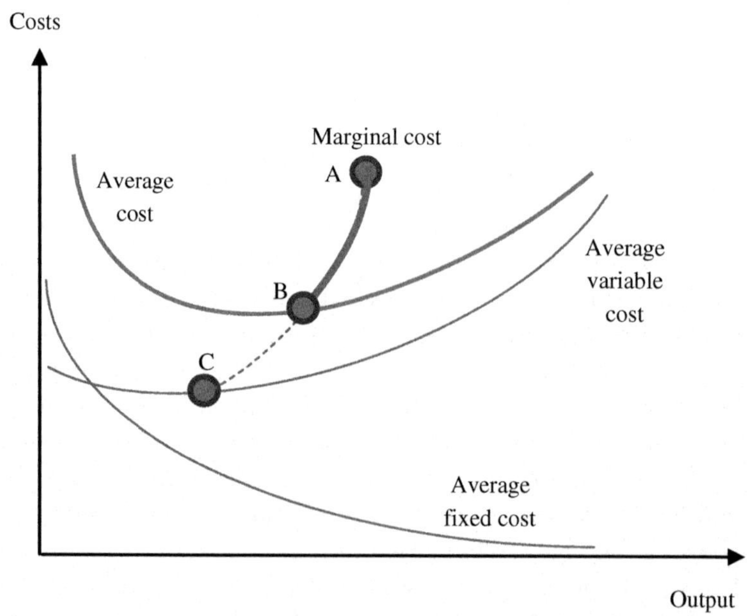

Fig. 1.6 The supply curve

1.3 Imperfections

The framework discussed so far has an appealing attractiveness to it, with smooth lines and high competition preventing companies from inflating their prices overly. Politicians will often aim to increase competition as a means to make consumers better off and its electorate happier in the process. However, vested interests are sometimes able to lobby for the reverse, or it might not be possible to introduce competition in some areas. At these times, a monopoly or oligopoly may exist, where the company has more pricing power and therefore ceases to take the price from the market merely.

1.3.1 Non-competitive Markets

A monopoly exists when a single company dominates its market. As is the case in a competitive market, it will seek to produce at the level where its expected marginal costs equal the marginal revenue. However, the monopolist can exploit its power to set prices without being undercut by a competitor. As a result, the market price will be above the marginal cost for this level of output. How responsive demand is to that market price will determine what degree of markup it can get away with to maximise profits.

When a monopolist exploits its pricing power to restrict production and raise the price, there is real harm. Of course, the monopolist benefits by getting more money for each unit sold, albeit with a possible offsetting loss in the additional sales it could have made at a lower price. That gain and loss are areas "A" and "C" in Fig. 1.7, where the former is essentially a transfer of well-being from consumers, who would have preferred to pay the lower price that would have prevailed in a competitive market. Meanwhile, area "B" is a loss to consumers who would have been willing to pay slightly more than the competitive market price, but not as much as has been marked up by the monopolist. Overall, the existence of a monopoly creates a welfare loss of B+C.

Monopolies do not run most markets in the real world, but the rest are not perfectly competitive either. This middle ground, where a few large companies can dominantly affect prices, is called an oligopoly. There are numerous different ways that oligopolistic businesses can interact. In general, though, we might think of an oligopoly as either having a leader or comprising companies that compete more equally in real time. Either way, the combined output will affect the market price while their relationship determines how the market balances out. Interesting theoretical games exist for

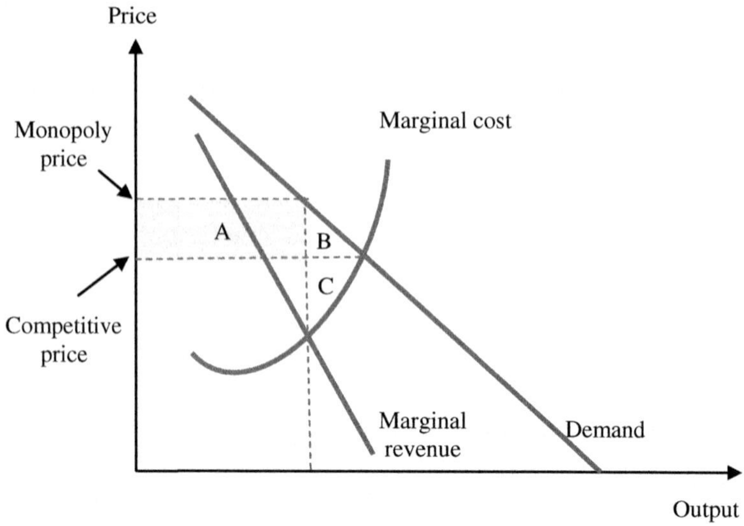

Fig. 1.7 Monopolistic welfare loss

various arrangements, typically simplified to involve only two companies. Unfortunately, this sort of exercise ends up so far away from reality that it would be quite a long and pointless cul-de-sac to explore here. For those of you who are interested, start by looking up the Stackelberg model and Cournot equilibrium. Just don't expect to be able to deploy what you find during real market investments.

1.3.2 Aggregation Problems

So far, this chapter has focused on the interactions of self-interested individuals and companies and some of the imperfections that can occur. Understanding such motivations can help us to anticipate what they might make of various developments. However, moving from this firmly microeconomic focus to a macroeconomic one is not entirely straightforward. It might seem like it is in a lot of academic material, but simple stories rely upon simplifying assumptions that are frequently glossed over. Sometimes the economy or markets might do things that don't seem logical because microeconomic motives are ignored, but sometimes the surprise may be because the microeconomic theory is itself overly simplistic.

For the demand of an individual to reflect the aggregated demand of all people in an overall market, some highly restrictive conditions need to hold. These so-called Sonnenschein-Mantel-Debreu conditions relate to how demand varies with income (the so-called Engel curve) between consumers. In short, the ratio of consumed goods must not be affected by income or differ between individuals. What these assumptions amount to is that market demand curves are only smooth and downward sloping when that is true of a "representative consumer", who everyone is identical too. That is, of course, nonsense, even if it might be a convenient approximation to ignore all idiosyncrasies of individuals. A real-world demand curve might have upward and downward sloping sections. Companies are ultimately observing points on the real curve and can build up an image of relevant portions that may not be perfect, but they allow businesses to form a better understanding of their market and what would be best for them to do. Simple stories grounded in the simplified theory might sound compelling and sometimes work, but we must not forget the underlying complexities, and be accordingly cautious.

1.4 National Accounting

Empirical observations assist companies to operate in their markets, and the same is true at the macrolevel. Stepping up to see the big picture requires data that aggregates all these interactions together into national accounts. Defining such data is no trivial task, though, with multiple approaches and fudge factors to fit it all together. Statistical manuals on such things can run to several hundred pages, but they serve primarily as points of reference. Reading one is a cure for insomnia, not a way to learn how the national accounts practically fit together. Forming fundamental views of the economy requires at least some familiarity with these data, though. Without data to provide evidence, any views could easily be invalid and any associated trades foolhardy.

National accounts aim to provide a comprehensive account of activity in an economy. The core measure for this is the gross domestic product (GDP). Other measures are arguably a better reflection of how citizens' living standards are evolving, but they are better for political point scoring then measuring market outlooks. There are three different ways to calculate GDP itself, with each delivering a different data breakdown to analyse. The core equivalence here is that output, expenditure and income in an economy are identical flows in each period. And where this activity is beyond (or beneath) the means of any sector, there is borrowing (or lending) that accumulates stock positions on their balance sheets. Exploring these areas of the statistical sausage factory, in turn, makes up the rest of this chapter.

1.4.1 Flows

Often the most reliable read on GDP growth in the short term comes from data on what firms are producing. Ask a manufacturing company this, and a clear answer about the value of the final products it produced is a relatively trivial question. Ask the same of a service sector company selling something with a definite price, and it is similarly simple. However, things can get a lot trickier. What is the value of something that has no market price?! The input cost of producing public services (including depreciation of fixed assets) is often the practical statistical solution for that sector. Alternatively, the results of that expenditure, like education results, might be used. Either way, it's a subjective mess. And financial services present additional challenges. Balance sheet size multiplied by an interest rate spread is treated as a core part of this activity, with fee-based bits the rest, but it is not entirely obvious that this is a fair measure of the actual value of the sector to the economy.

Ultimately, this "production approach" to GDP is trying to measure the gross value added (GVA) in the economy. The value added created at earlier stages of the production process must be subtracted to prevent double counting of the final value added, so the costs of these inputs are deducted as so-called intermediate consumption. The share of this intermediate consumption is not accurately measured in anything close to real time, hence the horrible lags in releasing the underlying "input/output, supply and use" tables. Between updates, this share is commonly assumed to be constant. That's fine until the economic cycle turns, which unfortunately is when the numbers matter most. The intermediates include things like advertising and other business-to-business trades that are inherently more cyclical than final output. Ignoring this can bias output estimates for years after turning points until more of the first fall and subsequent recovery in production becomes classed as intermediate rather than final gross value added. Bias can sometimes initially dominate in the other direction, though, because of smoothing forward growth from surveys that are slower to return actual numbers. Growing use of administrative data (e.g. tax returns) should shrink such problems over time, but one should nonetheless remain mindful of data fallibility.

Estimating GDP can also be approached using expenditure data, which can in turn tie back to the output sectors. The main types of expenditure that together equal GDP are private consumption, government consumption, investment and exports. Imports of goods and services are also subtracted here because we are after gross *domestic* product. Absent this deduction any foreign trade would be double counted globally, erroneously so on the purchaser's side. Consumption is more straightforward and includes most purchases you would personally make. That does not include purchases of durable assets (e.g. a house). Nor does it include payments of interest. As the government's consumption often lacks a market price, it is often assumed to equal the inputs, like procurement, staff costs and depreciation. Investment is a multifaceted beast better known statistically speaking as gross capital formation. The core part is in fixed assets, which are not used up in the production process. It's the same principle with net acquisitions of valuables like jewellery and art. And finally there is the change in inventories, whether that be of inputs, work in progress or final output. A brief exploration of the approaches to estimating all of these expenditure components is in Chap. 2.3.

Beside the output and expenditure approaches to measuring GDP, data on income can also be used to derive GDP from another perspective. Compensation of employees tends to be the biggest part, and it includes not only direct compensation as wages and bonuses but benefits in kind (e.g. company cars) and employers' pension and national insurance contributions. The gross trading profits that companies make on top of what they pay out to staff is the other main income type. Of course, some people are self-employed and so don't have income that neatly fits into these other boxes. For them, the income payable for employment and accrued as profits cannot be reasonably separated, so this is classed as "mixed income" instead. These three income types (employee income, profits and mixed income) are all measured on a cost basis, so the final addition to make GDP is to translate this into market prices by adding the net taxes on production and products. When an economy is spending more than it has earned, there is a deficit to finance. One sector's surplus might merely fund another's deficit, but when the economy as a whole is in deficit, the shortfall will need to be made up by other countries.

1.4.2 Accumulating Stocks

Flows of net lending and borrowing round off the income accounts, but their relevance does not end there. Lenders accumulate assets associated with their lending while the borrowers accumulate an equivalent liability. There are therefore four accumulation accounts dealing with changes in balance sheet positions. This concept is relevant to each sector, but the national position relative to the rest of the world tends to be the most discussed, with the current account balance of the balance of payments a particular focus. The current account covers goods and services trade with the rest of the world, current transfers (e.g. payments to supranational organisations, like the EU), and income on investments (e.g. dividends and coupons).

The financial account deals with what types of financial assets and liabilities are accumulating in exchange for the net lending made to an economy. Together with the investment income that this generates, there is arguably a self-reinforcing quality in the current account, where a surplus buys more foreign assets that in turn make an income and increase the balance or vice versa on the downside. In practice, other stuff tends to intervene to override this feedback loop, as Chap. 8 will explore. Some people find such flows dull, but others (usually FX strategists) have an obsession with the financial account that often appears to forget that the net accumulation of assets is related to savings in the economy. There is a borrower backed by any lending, so both sides are needed to tell the whole story. If you read one of the tediously detailed reports on capital flows, just remember to step back and see both sides of the economic wood rather than the many trees.

As net lending leads to an accumulation of assets and liabilities, the balance sheet will also be affected by price changes, which the revaluation account covers. It might be tempting to dismiss it because no financial transactions need take place at revalued prices, thereby preventing any associated gain or losses from being realised. However, that misses the confidence effect on savings decisions associated with the balance sheet health of each sector. As with the income accounting, those sectors include households, corporates (financial and non-financial), the public sector and the external one (i.e. international investment position). It is an especially tricky thing for statisticians to record who owes what to whom but attempts are increasingly being made to do this more and better. Such statistics can be quite helpful in identifying imbalances with the potential to trigger significant adjustments and thus trading opportunities. That is a topic for Chap. 3 though.

Main Messages

- Economics is about the allocation of limited resources to satisfy unlimited desires. At the core of it all is human action.
- Individuals seek to maximise their utility, subject to constraints. Their demand curve arises from their personal preferences in any situation.
- Increases in incomes and declines in prices are usually assumed to raise demand. Some goods are necessities with a demand that may rise with its price as consumption gets crowded in. It all depends on how individuals interpret its relative value to them.

- Companies face a variety of costs. Some vary with production and others are fixed for different lengths of time. The cost of producing an additional unit is known as the marginal cost.
- When the marginal cost of production equals the marginal revenue from its sales, a competitive company will maximise its profits.
- Monopolies have more pricing power to impose a markup. By preventing sales that could have otherwise profitably occurred at slightly lower prices, the welfare of consumers can be harmed.
- Idiosyncrasies of individuals mean real-world demand curves are often so much more complicated than simplified microeconomic models make out, owing to their nonsensical reliance on a single representative consumer.
- The national accounts record activity in an economy from an output, expenditure and income perspective. Data for all broad approaches are fallible, especially around economic turning points, when they are most needed.
- Where a sector or nation's expenditure exceeds its income, borrowing occurs. Tracking the resultant international capital flows is a favoured pastime of many analysts, but we should not miss the wood for the trees. Such financial transactions also have a counterpart in net savings.

Further Reading

Eurostat. 2010. *European System of Accounts—ESA 2010*. Luxembourg: Publications Office of the European Union.

Keen, Steve. 2011. *Debunking Economics: The Naked Emperor Dethroned?*. Zed Books.

Office for National Statistics. 1998. *UK National Accounts: Concepts Sources and Methods*. London: The Stationery Office.

Varian, Hall. 2010. *Intermediate Microeconomics: A Modern Approach*. W. W. Norton & Company.

2

Real Activity

While the first chapter explained the concepts underlying levels of demand and supply, it focused on the *what* and *why* rather than the *how*. Beyond willingness, the ability to pay is needed to make these levels possible. Ability arises from production, while willingness determines the exchange value of that. Producing something no one wants does not improve general living standards. Nor does an individual's standard of living necessarily benefit from a larger number of people creating things, even though this mechanically raises demand in the economy. Ultimately, living standards depend on being able to produce more for less—i.e. productivity. Unfortunately, this is a difficult thing to explain, let alone forecast, yet we must do so, albeit only implicitly in many cases.

It is about here where we must move increasingly from a focus on activity levels to growth rates. An economy simply cannot grow sustainably without productivity. And the choice of what productive projects to pursue will determine an economy's dynamic path. These dynamics matter in real markets. When it comes to modelling and monitoring some of the core activity growth measures though, we must bring in other factors. Doing so for the main expenditure components as well as the labour market delivers an applied end of this chapter. Labour supply and its productivity are not always apparent in that, but as a core part of the economic system, they are everywhere important.

P. Rush, *Real Market Economics*,
https://doi.org/10.1057/978-1-349-95278-6_2

2.1 Labour Supply

It is tempting to see the supply of labour as a predetermined irrelevance—literally what we're born with—but that does not mean it is a constant through time and geographies. Time waits for no one, and as it passes, the structure of the population changes. Moreover, the path of each area is broadly beholden to its historical structure. Such structures for people are what we dub demographic profiles. With different demographic groups having distinguishing characteristics, this stuff can matter a lot in many ways. Indeed, it even helps drive the average number of hours offered for work, which is the other side of the labour supply story.

2.1.1 Demographics

At its core, demographics are about births and deaths. Both must befall everyone walking the earth. And yet although the occurrence is a rare certainty to latch on to, the timing is much less clear. Few people can time the delivery of their baby according to a plan conceived earlier in life, and fewer still know when they will die. Fortunately, this is one area where individual behaviour is usually independent enough that across the full population, births and deaths can be reasonably close to forecasts on average. It is as though the individual errors cancel each other out.

As part of mechanically modelling population ageing—for those inclined not just to accept official versions—the fertility and death rate for each cohort are crucial. The former is usually a personal decision influenced by what is biologically possible, economically viable and socially normal. All have served to shift peak fertility rates later. Medical advances have made it safe to give birth much later while lower infant mortality discourages large family units. Meanwhile, the high costs of raising children and completing extended schooling have made it unaffordable to have children while young. A larger pool of potential partners plus contraception has also made it socially normal to start families later and, in many places, socially acceptable to eventually form families multiple times over with successive partners.

Death rates for most cohorts have been declining, often owing to variants of the same factors. Most directly, medical advances have cured various mortal ailments, but they have also prolonged life expectancies for those afflicted and made many conditions less debilitating. Meanwhile, vaccinations and general hygiene reduce incidence of illness. Economic development is, in turn, making all of this affordable. Moreover, the process of development takes people away from hard labours where at-work mortality is higher, towards work that is anyway less physically taxing. Broader provision of pensions and insurance products has also reduced the risk of destitution. And as backstops from the state have become more socially acceptable, this risk has been shrunk still further, lowering death rates with it.

Government policy can also have a more direct effect. Extremist politicians and other groups have at times sought to "cleanse" characteristics they consider undesirable, like different ethnicities and religions or disabilities. Such extreme policies typically emerge from situations beyond the extremes experienced in most of the developed world nowadays. Unfortunately, that is not the case everywhere, with parts of the Middle East and Africa still suffering significantly. Less discriminate measures like China's one-child policy can also have effects and not just through the direct incentive they place on birth numbers and thus the age distribution. The gender balance can skew because of how controls interact with cultural preferences, like parents wanting male heirs to help care for them in old age. That can set up a future lull in birth rates owing to an insufficient number of childbearing age women. Even countries like the UK are not immune to this, with a male skew developing despite children not needing to provide for their parents and only modest policy-induced incentives for small families. Importation of a cultural gender preference appears to have occurred through migration.

More generally, migration is an equaliser. Moving one's life is not normally done on a whim. A prospect of the quality of life improving is needed, with people pushed away from repressive regimes and weak economies with high unemployment or simply low wages. And because it is a decision about moving from one area to another, these factors are all relative. Indeed, the wealthiest in the world are also among the most internationally mobile as they chase higher or safer after-tax returns on their capital and labour. The usual frictions against migration like relocation costs and prolonged separation from networks also apply less. Meanwhile, the recipient country will likely be more welcoming of those with the means to more than pay their way.

Low-skilled migration is not without economic merit too, as this can allow more efficient job matching for other workers and generate increased output and expenditure that will fund further jobs. Large proportional remittances to home countries can curtail that effect though, especially in currency areas where exporters will struggle to benefit from the corresponding depression of the exchange rate. And the benefits of migration are anyway much smaller on average per person than for the overall economy. For the public who assess and vote on their personal experience, the societal costs tend to be much more tangible, thereby stoking opposition to low-skilled migrants. Some societies are naturally less welcoming than others though, especially if they fear cultural dilution. Explicit emphasis by some politicians on multiculturalism rather than being multiracial may not help either.

It is not just structural factors like the above that drive migration. Absolute and relative economic performance oscillates, and in these cycles, the attractiveness of countries can change, encouraging inward or outward movement in the process. And migration is not the only cyclical demographic driver. Birth rates can be pro-cyclical, essentially because babies are expensive. Likewise for divorces, which are even more pricey. Even death rates are sometimes cyclical when competition from a booming economy sucks away skilled support staff in health care. In other circumstances, though, cyclical cutbacks by squeezed governments or insurance payers could raise mortality risk—no suicidal tendencies are needed.

While demographics are affected in various ways by the economic cycle, they also feed back into it. Productivity and saving are the two main channels for this. The former arises from the accumulation of useful skills and efficiencies with extra years' experiences. These qualitative elements boost the productivity of workers and make higher pay affordable. However, saving for retirement can take up much of this additional income, driving financial asset prices in the process. It is rational for individuals to do this so that their consumption profile is smoother through time. Sharp cutbacks caused by a shortage of savings to run down in retirement (or unemployment) are a recipe for a relatively miserable time. In practice, most people do not deprive themselves to the extent necessary to fund anywhere near the same level of disposable income in retirement. They focus much more on fulfilling immediate needs. And that myopia transcends into the amount of work done and desired.

2.1.2 Hours Offered

For most people, employment is a means to an end and that end is not working a particular number of hours. The aim is instead to enjoy the highest standard of living they can attain. Of course, a big part of life is work itself, so being in enjoyable employment matters in addition to the compensation it offers. Moreover, it is tough to be successful in a job you don't enjoy, but then it is also true you can't be paid well in a job whose commercial value means it cannot pay well. Broadly speaking, there is a trade-off between work and leisure that each person must make. That trade-off is not a linear one though, not least because of significant discontinuities arising from what is feasible.

When people tell a statistician they want to work more hours, what most mean is that they want to take home more money, perhaps because their cost of desired living has increased. There is more than one way to do that. Those other options also tend to become more prevalent in a stronger environment when more hours are available too. Most obviously, competition for workers will be driving up pay in an active market, directly delivering what is ultimately wanted. Alternative jobs with more enticing salaries will also appear, allowing a compensation uplift from changing employer rather than changing hours. What this tends to mean is that people are ultimately satisfied with a smaller rise in hours than they might themselves think they need.

In addition to the shocks above on the cost of living side, numerous other things can affect the number of desired working hours from the returns to work side. These loosely comprise the various tax and allowance rates on employment versus the benefits available. Together, a net withdrawal rate is calculable for an individual considering working an additional hour. The interaction of the various allowances and benefits is frequently overlooked though, which leads to large discontinuities in the withdrawal rates faced. Perversely, removal rates can actively penalise additional work. Fixing this so that work would always pay was the aim of the UK government when it ambitiously sought to wrap up various benefits into a "Universal Credit". Even then, it set the cap at about 65%. The prospect of only being able to take home 35% of any additional earned income is arguably not that attractive, but its a lot better than what it used to be in the UK and what remains in some other countries.

Intrusive tax and benefits can go so far as to disrupt the decision about whether to participate in the labour market at all—i.e. the desired number of hours falls to zero. The return of any work beyond the benefits on offer would essentially be below the value of a life of leisure. That balance should become more skewed towards leisure near retirement age too, as there are fewer years of potential work ahead to lose by exiting the labour force. Retirement is also influenced by regulation and the standard of living affordable afterwards. In addition to any public pension entitlement, that means privately held pensions and assets. Accumulated capital must generate enough of an income alongside the consumption of the capital itself to fund the full retirement.

The risk of outliving one's assets means many de-risk their portfolio to the point of buying an annuity income. From that perspective, it becomes apparent that when long-term real yields are low, only a lower standard of retirement becomes affordable, which encourages continued employment. Health can be a particular factor here but can be a problem more generally.

Severe disabilities can make some or all types of work impossible. Lesser impairments might merely harm physical or mental productivity. And even when the potential employee is willing and able, an employer's fear of losing sunk training costs with a future retiree might make it harder for them to find a job anyway. There are many different types of treatment to various disabilities that are aiding participation though. And applied to healthy individuals too, there are potentially bigger benefits for the economy as a whole from adopting some of these advances.

2.2 Productivity

An enlarged workforce directly raises potential output, but it can also support the output of each worker by creating more room for them to find jobs that better match their skill set. There are many other ways output per worker (productivity) can be enhanced though. And these are real drivers of improved living standards. Individuals can choose to take actions that boost their lot through self-improvement. That mostly means education, but other things are addressed here that may be of a more personal interest to you, given what a competitive bunch market participants are. Beyond self-improvements, there are the investments in innovations that provide workers with external support. However, not all investment is equal in the same way that people are not identical to each other or even to themselves through their lives. There is thus a qualitative aspect to what the stock of capital and labour can produce. It is the entrepreneurial instincts of individuals that make the difference here, which takes us back to you.

2.2.1 You ++

Investment in a human context is most commonly considered to be education, education and education. Numerous studies have shown strong financial returns from further stages of education. An aim to extend such benefits has motivated the policy of many governments. So there has been an upward creep in the number of years young people are forced to stay in formal education for, with strong direction beyond that towards attending a university. However, there are uneven returns to education between individuals and subjects. Qualitative characteristics of the education matter as well as the quantity. Rising graduate unemployment and underemployment (i.e. work in areas not needing the extra education) are signs this training may not have been advisable in all circumstances. Human capital can thus be wasted in education too. So while training is typically helpful, raising productivity is not as simple as increasing graduations. A real need must exist rather than just state intervention.

Education can be provided outside of official institutions too and need not be structured towards any formal qualification to raise productivity. Indeed, this book is one such example amid an increasingly widespread availability of useful ideas. Unfortunately, people also appear to be suffering from an information overload that is shortening attention spans and hollowing out deep thoughts. Financial market participants have not been immune to this trend either. Short bursts of brain training exercises have become popular methods of speeding cognitive function, but these are arguably mainly about improving reactions to specific and arbitrary tasks. There have also been some promising signs of cognitive enhancement through directly training the brain by both transcranial magnetic and electrical stimulation. Ambitious attempts are being made to take this to another level, with brain-machine interfaces, which would be revolutionary if achieved.

A less niche and less contentious but more controversial development is the invention of "smart drugs"—i.e. pharmacological cognitive enhancements. Some of these have been around for decades and designed for officially approved solutions to cognitive problems, like attention deficit disorder and narcolepsy. That helps maximise the productive potential of people with those conditions. However, as those with normal or high baseline cognitive function usually attain even higher levels when consuming such drugs, potential benefits are more widespread. Most notably, Modafinil and its more refined successor, Armodafinil (among others), can cause improved cognitive flexibility and focus. Methylphenidate is more focused on improving working memory, but the increased concentration of dopamine it causes can be counterproductively addictive. None comes close to the sort of drug at the centre of films like limitless, or at least not yet. Nonetheless, it is possible for those with the means and willingness to buy a small but significant advantage. Widespread public adoption does not appear at all imminent though. Politicians do not want to condone any method of reinforcing inequality or force voters to take anything with potential side effects for the sake of keeping up with so-called biohackers.

The biohacking movement also embraces the field of epigenetics in a search for how to optimise the active and inactive genes (i.e. the phenotype not genotype). Unlike pharmacological steps though, epigenetics affects everyone, it is just that most people take a broadly passive approach to it. And even for those who don't, phenotype changes can be inherited. Small changes can also have unforeseen effects because of the complex epistatic interaction of two or more genes. Research in this relatively new area holds promise mainly regarding how to reduce disease incidence. In the interim, well-meaning changes or independent environmental factors will continue to drive change. And they may not be the desired ones. Unhealthy dieting fads can impede physical well-being, including through breeding dietary intolerance. Meanwhile, bad stress fixated on things that lack a productive end appears to be mounting. For example, there seems to be more generalised social anxiety as people look into the lives of others through an unrealistically rose tinted window on platforms like Facebook. Stress targeted to dissatisfaction with an aspect of one's mind or body can instead lead to training that brings real and healthy changes. What effects will dominate over different points in time remains to be seen, but increasing knowledge in this area will hopefully help.

Whereas cognitive enhancements and epigenetics are not readily observable and thus easily ignored, physical improvements have been evident. Replacement limbs have boosted mobility to the point that superior strength and speed are possible than with natural ones. Meanwhile, exoskeletons have progressed to a point where they are starting to become useful in heavy industries, albeit with some bugs and cost currently constraining adoption. Sensory enhancement is similarly moving far beyond the bulky hearing aids and glasses of old. Laser eye surgery has long been able to correct even minor imperfections. Augmented reality glasses will soon be able to take the sense of sight to a new level of smartness. Overlaying useful information into the field of view leaves hands free for other things, and to the extent it anticipates needs, they will make users appear "smarter" by extension. Other implants could assist in this by feeding in their situational data. There is no shortage of advances in the pipeline that will aid people's inherent productivity.

2.2.2 Help for Humans

All of the above advances have been about maximising one's personal productivity. However, there is a world of developments outside of ourselves. One relatively new example of this is the field of collective cognition, where tools combine the decisions of many individuals to create a whole that is better than the sum of its parts. Google's PageRank search algorithm is a good example of this. It aims to ascertain what the most suitable search result is using knowledge of what pages satisfied previous searchers.

This system can deliver superior results for less time hunting. Similarly, smart client relationship management (CRM) systems can allow for a better targeted and quality of customer coverage by identifying gaps and common interests on which to focus resources.

New systems to extract information from activity for other applications are arising in numerous areas. Online marketplaces are an example that is already well established in many countries. Such platforms lower the costs of launching products and services to buyers, partly by making it more efficient to find buyers. The same is also increasingly true for financial products via peer-to-peer debt and equity platforms, although they remain minnows in comparison with the whales of the established banking system. Other peer-to-peer platforms have been more successful where they essentially allow the flexible rental of assets, including time. Such flexibility aids in the maximisation of productivity by those assets, which is the essence of the so-called sharing economy, controlled by the likes of Uber and Airbnb in cars and residences, respectively.

Market structures are evolving to include these online and "sharing" platforms. Both are beneficial for making markets complete, which should ultimately support the efficient allocation of investment. Markets help keep prices aligned with the balance of broader preferences, thereby meaning prices are more reliable signals for production. An investment that results might be for tangible (physical) assets, like machines and factories, or in intangible ones like intellectual property (e.g. patents and trademarks). Together, these are the kinds of capital seen as raising productivity and thus encouraged by governments. Sometimes the state intervention is of the relatively benign and indiscriminate type, letting real markets decide what investment is best. However, all too often interventions are targeted at pet projects on the assumption that all investment is good and equal, which is patently untrue.

2.2.3 Malinvestment

In reality, the stock of capital in an economy takes myriad forms with hardly any of it similar enough to offer a suitable substitute. In the economists' lingo, real capital is heterogeneous and rarely fungible. Even when a particular part of the capital stock has a perfect replacement, there is still an intricate latticework of uniquely structured capital underlying the overall stock. Innovation is needed to make the most valuable combination, and that is the realm of an entrepreneur. Naturally, many of those innovations are unable to fulfil genuine demands at a profitable price and are thus destined to fail. Propping them up is a recipe for distorting signals and ultimately misaligning production and consumers' real needs, creating a welfare loss. Worse still, the whole latticework of capital can be corrupted in the process, magnifying the size of any future correction back towards meeting customer's real preferences. In that adjustment, even new and functioning capital can become wasted if it is impossible to transform to new requirements.

Neither distributed ownership models nor collective cognitive decisions are a cure to errors. What might initially appear rational in the short term can easily prove not to be, especially when an investment's viability relies on a government intervention. Moreover, markets can become manic as investors herd into the same area. As it is almost tautological to describe the crowd's group think as collective cognition, there is a reason to think such advances could compound the misallocation of capital (malinvestment) as technology advances in this area. To the extent that occurs, bigger imbalances can accumulate ahead of larger adjustments (more on this in Chap. 4). The existence of an imminently correcting imbalance might only be apparent after sentiment has turned and the unwind becomes visible. In both stages, there will be an effect on the composition of the utilised capital structure. If it is a part that has an inherently high (or low) level of productivity, there will be a shock to whole economy productivity growth.

There can be highly persistent effects on productivity from where resources flow, especially when large loans lever the purchaser's income. Perhaps the most obvious example of this is in housing, but it can apply to other existing assets. The problem there arises from the asset having no additional productive return on the investment. After all, a house providing a standard of shelter before a transaction will also do so after a sale at a higher price. Where demand has bid up the price against sticky supply though, economic resources fall into an inefficient cul-de-sac from which no real growth can emerge to pay for its financing. Price inflation might still make the investment profitable for the individual, but it is counterproductive for the economy as a whole. Writ large, such malinvestments can starve the real economy of the real resources it needs to deliver real economic growth in the future.

2.3 Forecasting Real Growth

Demographics and the underlying productivity performance are the big structural stories driving long-term economic trends. Quantifying them in real time is not a trivial task though and translating the underlying trends into expectations for their actual values in each quarter is impractical. There are better ways to forecast the economy's cycle over the next couple of years, even though they are relatively ill-suited to the longer term trends. As most market participants only care about the shorter horizon, we shall focus there, while remaining mindful of the underlying trends driving direction. Meanwhile, the other economic variables estimated along the way can provide additional uses in ultimately understanding what will move real markets.

In the broadest terms, short-term forecasts should be done from the demand side of the economy, rather than based on what the economy's productive factors can supply, which had been the focus earlier in this chapter. As described in Chap. 1.4, demand in the economy can be calculated based on output, expenditure or income data. They are necessarily equal. In practice, an expenditure-based approach is the optimal way of forecasting growth over the next year or two. As horizons lengthen though, the forecaster must pay increasing heed to trends on the supply side and to those imbalances with the potential to prompt breaks from this framework. Meanwhile, income data feed into the expenditure outlook via the labour market and provide a good sanity check on forecasts. Output data can be another cross-check but are often at their best for tracking short-term economic performance. Such tracking is a task they are supported in by many output surveys from the private sector, with the practical aspects of doing so rounding off this chapter.

2.3.1 Domestic Demand

Most of a country's gross domestic product (GDP) is from its domestic demand. In some small open economies, external demand may be large enough to make exports bigger, but a small open economy's reliance on imports would also likely be large enough to shrink net trade's share of GDP. The government's expenditures can amount to more than 50% of GDP, but much of that is a redistribution of income that others then spend. The level of final expenditure that the government makes on its citizens' behalf is naturally a political decision. Meanwhile, the relative shares of investment and consumption, in the long run, are ultimately related to the country's production structure. There can be considerable variability in the national consumption and investment intensity, but private consumption is usually the largest part of that domestic demand.

Conveniently, given its centrality to any model of the macroeconomy, it is relatively easy to specify a well-fitting consumption function. Household income funds most household spending, and the majority of any change in real wage growth will translate into real consumption. Wealth is also used to finance some spending, so large changes in asset prices feed back into the real economy. Outright asset sales are not always possible or pursued though, especially for illiquid housing wealth. Nonetheless, the money tied up in these assets influences households' perceived financial stability and future consumption prospects. This and confidence more generally, proxied by things like unemployment rates, affects how much of any additional income households want to save and how much leverage to carry. Moreover, manipulation of interest rates can encourage some spending to be brought forward or delayed, contrary to underlying desires. This manipulation is the core component of cyclical demand management policy nowadays such that it is the subject of Chap. 6.

Similarly affected by interest rates is investment spending. Different maturity rates may be relevant, and the corporates making the investment might have a different risk profile, but that is a matter of price rather than economic principle. However, interest rates are a market quantum with a different relevance for corporates, as they can also sell equity privately or on a public exchange. Chief financial officers (CFOs) must determine how best to raise funds, taking into account investor interest across the company's capital structure. The potential operational returns from an investment are weighable against the various available funding costs. Fixed investment is thus encouraged when investors attach a high market value to a company's tangible assets. When spare productive capacity abounds though, it may still make more sense to utilise existing assets more instead of buying new ones, where both can raise the book value of assets. Each is essentially a response to a low price of investment where a low price relative to labour sends a similar signal.

A level of production beyond final demand creates additional inventory. Some level of stocks is almost always desirable as it allows for unanticipated increases in demand to be profitably satisfied. As there is a cost to storing and financing inventory, in addition to the risk of depreciation or outright obsolescence, inventory levels can also be too high. The rise of just in time delivery structurally lowered desired inventory levels but transport times over global supply chains and the risk of small disruptions forming bottlenecks means there is a limit to this. Beyond such structural considerations, inventory changes often move with the economic cycle, with shocks difficult to predict. Forecasting and analysing inventories are also complicated in Europe (and elsewhere) by the bundling into them of an "alignment adjustment" that squares total expenditure with overall output. A significant adjustment is a sign of data inconsistency that revisions may eventually resolve. Until then, markets are potentially being misguided about underlying economic strength.

Government consumption and investment at least sound like they should be easy to factor into a forecast. After all, politicians can be quite explicit in saying what they will do and by their size and legal dominance, they can deliver. In practice, there are difficulties even in assessing the direct effect of an expenditure plan. Measured outputs do not always equal the proposed inputs, and it is not always straightforward how an expenditure change scores as prices versus volumes. Even when the direct evidence is clear, care in interpreting it is needed. A good economist will embrace the hidden opportunity costs arising from what the monies might have bought if the government did not reappropriate them instead. And indirectly, the so-called multiplier effect of government spending on to expenditure elsewhere in the economy is one of the most contested areas of economics. Fiscal policy is thus worthy of a chapter unto itself. Indeed, it is this book's seventh.

2.3.2 External Trade

Domestic expenditure often contains an imported element, which must be subtracted to give a fair representation of the value added to production by each nation. As the import intensity of each type of expenditure is relatively stable over standard horizons, there is a strong correlation between import-weighted demand and imports. Forecasting imports in this way is also consistent. Measurement errors and only periodic updates of the import content data mean the relationship is not perfect. However, updating weights with each release of the "supply and use tables" means they should stay close. A similar weighting by import intensities of foreign demand, or at least by the share of exports going to the relevant country, is also possible. Standard cyclical patterns occur in the external trade data, and this contributes to economic cycles converging between countries. Shared structural trends in export and import shares also arise from nations specialising in areas of comparative advantage and removing protectionist barriers to trade.

Protectionism is a political response to popular pressure, despite it not being in the interest of consumers or the wider economy. Many forms exist beyond just taxing imports directly through tariffs, especially since trade agreements have clamped down on such levies. Non-tariff barriers include minimum standards regulations that fit and thus favour domestic producers, with environmental ones being a current favourite. Nor is this just or even mostly an issue for trade in goods. Even in notionally free trade areas like the EU, practical barriers are constraining the services sector. Consumers lose out from protectionism because access to the most efficient producer of the goods and services they demand is impeded, leaving them to face higher costs. At least in the short term, the benefit is only felt by the companies (and their stakeholders) shielded from competition. Resisting the specialisation of an economy prevents national wealth from being maximised pursuing its comparative advantage.

Protections are only one factor that influences the global competitiveness of companies, which reflects in their relative prices. Some of this price difference is simply the difference in domestic production costs. That is the underlying comparative advantage at work. Much more volatile is the trade-weighted exchange rate, as large movements in it facilitate a price adjustment without a painfully rapid reallocation of real resources. Or in other words, competitiveness can be quickly regained by a relative cut in all local prices rather than by lowering the production costs of everything for sale. Unfortunately, the quick fix does not resolve the real reason for a country losing competitiveness so repeated devaluations can become the norm.

2.3.3 Labour Market Activity

Activity in the real economy requires workers, so more workers would allow companies to increase their output. The wage earned by those workers can then be spent, in turn creating additional demand for the economy that justifies new employees. That is not to say hiring is always rational for the company doing it though, as most the demand will fall elsewhere. The marginal revenue earned from the extra output has to be higher than the cost of paying that worker. One justification for government intervention is therefore that it might be able to encourage enough employment and thus spillover effects ("externalities") to make the hiring collectively worthwhile. It is far from clear cut though (see Chap. 7).

The relationship between output and the number of workers hired to produce it means that employment can be forecast reasonably well using GDP growth. A little lag just needs to be allowed for because of the time it takes companies to decide they need the staff, find and then complete suitable hires. This relationship is Okun's law. Although it does well, especially in the short term, it is not a law. The amount of employment needed depends on what parts of the economy are expanding. As such, calibrating the "law" over long periods can cause persistent periods of over or underestimating the pace of employment growth. Inevitably, economists with poorly calibrated models will rush to brand such errors in the labour intensity of output as "productivity puzzles". It is usually just another instance of incorrectly assuming everyone is the same and thus able to produce an equivalent level of output.

A more payback prone sort of employment error is when labour has been hoarded or aggressively shed. The former typically occurs when businesses anticipate that any shortfall in demand they are facing is too temporary to warrant reducing headcount. Letting staff go is an expensive event in itself, and hiring is an even more expensive one once the cost of training and team assimilation are factored in. When the labour market is short of people looking for work, those costs are unusually high, so hoarding usually occurs when unemployment is low near cyclical peaks. Some commentators will try and argue it is happening at other times too though, even when it is intellectually inconsistent to do so, as was the case in the UK during the 2008 credit crunch (see Case study: Phantom labour hoarding). Any excuse for looser policy will do for some people. In contrast, aggressive shedding of employees occurs when rehiring costs are small compared to the risk of going out of business. This scenario is thus more of an issue when unemployment is high, and credit conditions are tight. Maximising discounted future profits then boils down to cost control as the driver of corporate behaviour.

Case study: Phantom labour hoarding

During the 2008 credit crunch, most UK economists argued that employment had held up much better than GDP because companies were hoarding workers. Such hoarding would leave them with the capacity to swiftly expand output as the economy recovered. Indeed, the economy's recovery could be jobless because no hiring was needed to meet additional production plans. Ultimately, the opposite happened, with the recovery being very jobs-intensive. However, this was entirely rational for companies under the circumstances. By definition, a credit crunch starves businesses of credit. To keep costs elevated by hoarding workers was to increase the risk of going bankrupt. There is no point saving the capacity to expand rapidly in a recovery if hoarding means the business is no longer trading by the time that recovery comes. So the labour hoarding hypothesis was intellectually inconsistent with the fundamentals of a credit crunch. An understanding of real markets made the opposite outcome possible to forecast profitably.

Not all employees have much say in the number of hours they work at a given job, but many have some power, even if it might mean moving jobs. If both the employees and their employer want to work for more hours on average, this can be a suitable substitute to hiring additional workers. It is thus a form of labour hoarding to keep such desires primed for fulfilment in the future. Manufacturing companies are particularly prone to take this approach, with shifts shortened or cancelled during downturns. Germany even has state subsidised schemes with this in mind that moderate recessionary rises in unemployment. As additional average hours are easier to come by in a strong labour market, the two are positively related. However, it is far from perfect with workers who want to work fewer hours also in a better bargaining position to achieve it when the market is strong. Moreover, because an active labour market supports hourly pay, people can work less and fund a longer leisure time without financial loss. People want to be remunerated better rather than work extended hours for the sake of it, so when compensation improves, people are often satisfied with fewer hours than they might have previously said they preferred. For this reason, desired hours data are a poor predictor of what average hours will be in future. Much better in the short term are data on usual hours, which can highlight when holiday patterns are temporarily distorting the averages.

Amid offsetting cyclical effects, hours is not an easy thing to forecast. Separate structural trends can easily dominate here and also for participation in the labour market. In particular, demographic trends can drive changes in both. For example, people who lose their job near to retirement might decide it is not worth or possible to return to the labour market before they originally planned to retire, so start it early instead. Or they might choose to phase their way into retirement by becoming part-time or self-employed. At the other end, there is also the participation decision of would be students, where further education is more attractive in a weak labour market. Looking at movements in hours and participation rates for prime working age people is one simple way around the problem. Combining the hours/participation of different cohorts using stable weights, thereby fixing the demographic profile at a given moment, makes an approximate adjustment for demographic effects. It often becomes a highly contentious matter of judgement though where different people will draw different conclusions from the same data, sometimes with high conviction in opposing directions. A cautious approach is arguably best in this area.

2.3.4 Tracking Your View

Irrespective of what view you hold on how the economy will evolve, its formation is not the end of the matter. How well incoming data conform to it will determine how you manage any associated investments. Hopefully, the view is correct and will thus find corroboration from incoming data. This evidence can, in turn, build conviction around the idea, potentially encouraging more capital to be placed at risk in its name, if the market has not already priced out any profitable opportunities. Of course, it's not possible to be right all the time, and it is just as important to know when that is the case. Data that challenge the view must lower conviction levels, and this would in effect raise the amount of risk any associated investment carries. Unwinding some of the investment is needed to rightsize the risk of it with the strength of the underlying view's conviction. This approach is the economic underpinning for the logic of letting your profits run and cutting your loses, which is a big part of successful investing.

There are so many data releases to dig into that a very boring book could be written on them alone. Fear not, that is not this book. Nonetheless, it is worth presenting a quick survey of the surveys, where most are exactly that. Respondents to surveys are not infallible and may not be representative, so standard errors around numbers can be wide. That applies both to official releases of national statistics and to the private surveys, despite the former potentially never being finalised and the latter never being revised. Plans are afoot to make fuller use of tax receipt data, which should make numbers more reliable by raising their coverage. However, this is not possible for all data, and there will still be some gaps and fallibility, intentionally or otherwise.

Despite their propensity for revision, official figures are conventionally referred to as "hard", opposed to the "soft" private surveys. Such hard data can be from the output, expenditure or income sides of the national accounts. Of output, the most high profile is industrial production, which encompasses the manufacturing, mining, utilities and sometimes construction sectors. Some countries have an index of services as well to give more detail on this side of the economy, which is typically much larger. Where monthly versions exist, they provide a more timely read on the economy than quarterly GDP and can be used to build a monthly GDP measure (e.g. Canada has an official one). Data on orders are patchy and more volatile but can guide on the outlook. Expenditure on imports of semi-manufactured goods can also be of use here. More generally, external trade data, together with retail sales and sometimes inventory or investment numbers (e.g. USA) provide an expenditure led perspective on the performance of the economy.

Regarding "soft" data, each country has numerous idiosyncratic releases. Of those that are comparable across a wide range of countries, by far the best are the purchasing manager indices (PMIs and the similar US ISM). Publication of these data occurs on the first few working days after month end, with many countries having so-called flash estimates released a bit earlier too. Like many surveys, they are diffusion indices, meaning they are a balance of up and down responses. Strictly speaking, this netting makes them indicators of breadth rather than the pace of growth but the two can be strongly correlated, albeit with some shocks driving a big wedge between the two. Problematic gaps can emerge between implied growth rates and their change in the hard and soft data. Sometimes revisions cause a convergence again, but differences can persist for a long time, leaving a lot of uncertainty about what the true story is in the interim. An understanding of differences in methodology and thus how they respond differently to shocks might help reconcile what is going on. Sometimes an inexplicable divergence is just that though.

Even when a large change in hard and soft data is real in the sense that it happened, it may not be macroeconomically significant. It may merely be noisy volatility rather than the start of a trend. Indeed, noise is often the explanation. Knowing what sorts of shocks are potentiality distorting the data at least allows for an investigation that can hopefully yield an estimate of what the underlying performance is. Some of them might even be predictable surprises, allowing those who bother with detail to beat the rest. For example, unseasonable weather conditions, changing seasonal factors for the economy, working day changes (including strikes) or sporting events, can all have considerable effects. Whether it be for identifying the size of these shocks or noise, looking at lower and different levels of aggregation can be an invaluable guide for gauging payback expectations.

In a short-term sense, it does not matter what the number released on the day is. If that figure is in line with the consensus of economists surveyed by Bloomberg and Reuters, market participants collectively shrug and move on. News in the details might be economically relevant but will struggle to find an audience and move the market quickly. That is why there are such stable elasticities between some data release surprises and market moves. However, where errors between data releases are considered correlated, the market will move the dial on where it thinks the consensus is such that a different one in effect exists. This adjustment is why market responses to some surprises can be relatively variable (e.g. services versus manufacturing PMIs), or hard to identify at all for data with earlier local releases (like German states informing expectations for the national and in turn the euro area's inflation rate).

For a release to drive longer term investment trends, the surprise has to be significant, normally by being unusually large. Surprises that tip the direction of data trends the wrong way can also carry additional weight. Essentially, it is the stuff that challenges investors' priors about the economy that matter. Good economists will align their research focus accordingly to where the real market moving news is. Unfortunately, there is still a deluge of dreary data coverage out there. Filtering out the monotonous stuff should help your sanity, whether you're on the receiving end of 10 irrelevant comments on a particular release or writing as many irrelevant comments each month. More importantly though, bypassing such tiresome tasks frees up some time to focus on the real market views that will reward your investment. And that's the stuff that matters here.

Main Messages

- The supply of labour and its productivity ultimately determine the level of economic activity. Labour is both headcount and hours worked, which are profoundly affected by the structure of domestic demographics and migration.
- Real improvement in an individual's standard of living comes from productivity. That can come from within (e.g. education) or from investment in suitably supportive equipment. And it does need to be suitable. Contrary to conventional assumptions, the allocation and type of resources available do matter.
- Forecasting the economic outlook for the next year or two is best done using expenditure data, which produces some market relevant details along the way. Income accounts provide a good cross-check, as do the supply side drivers.
- Domestic demand comprises the bulk of national output and is what policymakers have the most control over. Various versions of the relative price of current expenditure drive deviations away from what raw growth in real incomes indicates.
- Combining the growth of expenditure components using their import content provides a reliable and consistent estimate of import growth. Equivalently, export share weighted global demand determines exports. Foreign exchange rates are an important but secondary factor.

- The pace of GDP growth dictates the amount of additional labour (employees and hours) that are needed. Hoarding or excess shedding of employees is possible in response to temporary demand shocks in otherwise, respectively, strong or weak economic states.
- Tracking incoming economic data for consistency with your views is needed. The extent that data do (or don't) fit should raise (or lower) your conviction levels. As any associated investments will then carry less (or more) effective risk, those positions can be added to (or reduced), subject to market conditions.
- There are lots of data releases and even more details, which should not be mistaken for significance. Distortions are possible with all data, which have a margin of error. Weather, seasonal patterns, holidays and strikes are all examples of things to watch.

Further Reading

Brayton, Flint. Laubach, Thomas. Reifschneider, David. 2014. *The FRB/US Model: A Tool for Macroeconomic Policy Analysis.* FEDS Notes.

Burgess, Stephen. Fernandez-Corugedo, Emilio. Groth, Charlotta. Harrison, Richard. Monti, Francesca. Theodoridis, Konstantinos. Waldron, Matt. 2013. *The Bank of England's forecasting.*

Platform: COMPASS, MAPS, EASE and the suite of models. Working Paper No. 471. Bank of England.

Fagan, Gabriel. Henry, Jérôme. Mestre, Ricardo. 2001. *An Area-wide Model (AWM) for the Euro* Area. Working Paper No. 42. European Central Bank.

Hanke, John. Wichern, Dean. 2013. *Business forecasting.* Pearson.

Office for Budget Responsibility. 2013. *The Macroeconomic Model.* Briefing paper No. 5.

The Academy of Medical Sciences. 2012. *Human Enhancement and the Future of Work.* Report from a joint workshop hosted by the Academy of Medical Sciences, the British Academy, the Royal Academy of Engineering and the Royal Society.

3

Inflation and the Business Cycle

So far our focus has been on the volume of activity in the economy. Growth in the economy can come from these *real* factors or changes in average prices. Together, they amount to *nominal* economic growth. Such price changes are now conventionally known as inflation, though that was not classically the case. Measuring an average price is not as easy as it might seem, and capturing a realistic change in them is harder still. Resulting from this problem is a number intended to reflect the general experience of all yet actually representing the cost of living of no one.

Most price changes are anyway temporary ones as the best approach to seasonal demand is sought. The underlying rationale for trends in prices comes from cost pressures with a markup to make a profit. In both cases, there is an influence from the business cycle, where high competition for resources raises their price and gives companies the pricing power to demand a premium profit margin. There are also inflation expectations, where some mutually agreeable rate can embed in wages without necessarily raising costs if they can, in turn, be passed on to prices. Because these expectations sink into both wages and prices, there is potential for a feedback loop that causes a self-reinforcing wage-price spiral.

Anticipating an inflationary spiral is inherently challenging because of its nonlinearity. A little news can make no difference, or it might be the straw that breaks the camel's back. Perhaps more worrying is how little help economic theory is to forecast changes in the business cycle and its associated inflationary pressures. A critical weakness at the heart of mainstream models is partly to blame. Equilibrium is not the general and near steady state derived

P. Rush, *Real Market Economics*,
https://doi.org/10.1057/978-1-349-95278-6_3

from the flawed set of common assumptions. Nor are the policymakers following the recommendations of such models always the virtuous influence they assume, even if their intentions are benign. On the bright side, understanding the manipulated dynamics of the real economy creates an opening to outperform in real markets.

3.1 What Price

Before we can delve into the details of what drives price changes, we must understand what ones we mean. Nowadays we tend to talk about consumer prices as though they are a definite thing and the only meaning of "inflation", but it is not a straightforward thing to measure. Sampling restrictions and approaches to forming the index make all the difference to this approximate average. Nor has this focus on consumer prices always been the case. Classically, inflation was the growth in the quantity of money. That may sound odd, but it makes a lot of sense, even if it is also easy to get carried away with the usefulness of these money data.

3.1.1 Money Supply

It is a primary tenant of supply and demand to say that an increase in supply reduces the market clearing price. That same principle applies to money. When there is more money around, its price falls. With the value of money reduced, it will take more money to buy things. This reduction in the purchasing power is akin to growth in costs. If it is consumer goods and services prices rising, then this aligns with the modern term of inflation. However, this additional money need not flow to the consumer-facing sector. Prices will inflate wherever the money goes. More often than not that means asset prices. Existing holders of these assets benefit from a windfall that could motivate additional consumption, and thus price rises there. However, a relatively weak propensity for people to consume out of growth in financial wealth restricts this effect.

The notion that money growth reduces its purchasing power and thus raises prices is a nice simple story to keep in mind. It motivates us to hunt out where prices are growing and assess the significance of this even when nothing appears on a more conventional consumer price radar. Price changes are never uniform. What measure of money to use is itself a contentious issue even among those who still refer to such monetary aggregates.

The American tradition is to focus on the monetary base, which comprises the liabilities of the central bank (cash and reserve balances). This so-called high-powered money is levered up to make broader monetary aggregates. In practice, private banks are not usually short of this base money, so policies to increase it have no bearing on broader money measures. The so-called money multiplier merely falls.

British monetarists focus directly on the broader monetary aggregates dominated by private sector liabilities (e.g. M3 or M4). Doing so does not require a view on the money multiplier. However, its relevance to economic growth still needs money's so-called velocity of circulation to be relatively constant. This "velocity" is derived by dividing nominal GDP by the money supply and is thus the number of times this money is spent in the economy each year. Much of the money in the measure will lack the liquidity to be available immediately but is spendable with notice. For understanding money growth as the inflationary devaluation of the currency's purchasing power, this broader focus makes a lot more sense.

There is a third way being advanced by the Austrian economic school. Like the British monetarists, it values the breadth of coverage, but unlike it, this only covers the money that is available to spend immediately. Deposits that require notice before withdrawal, including mutual funds, are therefore dropped in the resultant "zero maturity" measures. Unfortunately, most countries do not cut the data this way, but many do provide a breakdown that makes it possible to create one. Perhaps unsurprisingly, focusing on the money available to spend now has a better fit with coincident economic data. There are more accurate ways of forecasting, but these money data can nonetheless provide a useful cross-check, if only for assessing risks.

3.1.2 Consumer Prices

Much more conventional in the contemporary debate is to treat inflation as solely about changes in the price of a basket of goods and services. As above, these prices need not move with the money supply. Forming a representative basket of such goods and services is not as easy as it sounds. A representative consumer must be defined, and its behaviour reflected. The breakdown of its consumption will be needed to weight together with the price of goods and services, which will evolve over time. New products and services will launch, while others end. Ignoring such changes in preferences is needed because they do not reflect an actual change in price. More controversial is the extension of this argument to quality improvements. Technological advances mean an identical product can be bought vastly cheaper in the future, but by then demand has switched to the replacement. Changes in the price of the new equivalent items rather than in the diminished legacy ones are still inflation (e.g. between new iPhone models, not always an original iPhone).

Ideally, changes in consumption patterns would be reflected in real time so that the change in actual prices paid would be known. However, the expense of getting such data even at relatively high levels of aggregation prohibits this from being a possibility. In practice, there is an annual weighting update instead. Blending prices using alternative weights over time would probably lead to a different headline number even if all underlying prices were unchanged. This remix would not be inflation so must not be conflated with actual price changes. Chain linking is the proper way around this. Each constantly defined series serves as a link that just reflects price changes. Interlinking them gives an overlap to combine otherwise different series into a consistent chain. Only price changes and not methodological breaks carry through, with revised weights not applied to old prices. However, delays in updating weights after significant relative price changes mean old weights will be used with new price changes for a time, biasing inflation numbers in the interim.

An additional problem is how to aggregate prices of things when no weights are known, as is the case between different types of apples. An average is needed, and the choice of the averaging method makes a big difference. Most common nowadays is to use a geometric average, which implicitly assumes that consumers substitute to the lower price items. That is reasonable between types of green apples in one store and less so between a green and red apple or between ones in different shops. It becomes downright nonsensical when applied to items fulfilling fundamentally different desires. A cooking apple does not become a substitute for a normal eating one when the latter goes up in price. Much more stretched examples exist in other areas.

Less sensitive to this excessively strong substitution assumption is an arithmetic average. However, in the place of this downward bias is arguably a bigger problem. If a price is cut in a sale and restored to its previous level afterwards, the arithmetic average of all the prices will be left higher than before the cut. This statistical property is clearly inconsistent with the underlying price changes and thus undesirable. An upward bias is especially undesirable for governments who are keen to report low inflation so that a given set of nominal data imply real standards of living improving to the maximum extent possible. So it should not be surprising that the state prefers measures with a downward bias in guidelines given to national statisticians.

3.1.3 Price Formation

Retailer behaviour has a big effect on the relative bias of the averaging approaches and measured inflation more generally. Much of this falls outside the normal realms of macroeconomic theory, but it drives most of the short-term movements in prices. Anticipating it requires detailed modelling of the transmission of price shocks, like to oil and other commodities, or the exchange rate. Companies are understandably loath to sell anything at a loss, but the jump between the major pricing points can cause wide variation in profit margins and price changes. Sometimes sales will be made as "loss leaders", with the intent that enough more profitable purchases are made elsewhere to compensate.

Sales can occur below average costs for as long as it can finance losses. However, the pricing strategy must target a suitably sustainable profit margin. If a company expects the marginal revenue of a sale to be less than the marginal cost of producing more, production has become unsustainable. This price puts a floor on prices. By extension, the balance of tail risks skews up as prices approach the marginal cost. Proximity to the effective floor will have shrunk downside room, while the upside potential increases. However, when a surplus in something with inelastic supply and demand causes the price fall, the downside tail, while trimmed in length, may appear more probable. That is because vast and persistent price changes are needed before supply responds to remove any surplus. When the surplus goes, there is a propensity for prices to overshoot as the production pipeline becomes based on the persistence of previously unsustainable prices. The result is periodic sharp switching between high- and low-price regimes.

As the structure of the competitive environment evolves, so too will the equilibrium level of profit margins. Transitioning between them will push a persistent change in the price level and a temporary one in inflation. Variations in the type of discounts being delivered also matter in this way because not all types of sales count. Typically, sales have to be openly available and be on price rather than volume. A 50% discount counts as disinflation, but a buy-one-get-one-free offer may not. Flash sales have the additional problem of probably missing the inflation survey, which usually uses an "index day" to collect prices around because of how costly and time-consuming the process is. Moreover, the use of online data remains rare, so the forum for most flash sales is missed.

The inflation data show strong seasonal patterns. Some of this is an attempt by retailers to attract demand when it is otherwise weak. Most of it is about clearing old stock, either because a new model is coming or because demand is itself seasonal. Clothing is a classic example of this behaviour. January sales dispose of some surplus winter stock ready for spring lines, and summer sales do the same for the autumnal lines. Subtle shifts in the thread count of the items also affect inflation because of the production costs and associated selling price changes. Some shops take this even further by purposefully stocking inferior quality products for sales periods with the sole intent of being able to offer them at what appears to be a deep discount.

To forecast or correctly interpret the implications of inflation data, an in-depth understanding of underlying seasonal behaviour is needed. This analysis must adjust for fundamental changes in behaviour over time and look through noise or a fleetingly different seasonal pattern. A variety of seasonal adjustment algorithms exists for doing this. Structural breaks in conduct and statistical methodology may need manual adjustment, or else surrounding seasonal factors will be biased. An algorithm cannot make large and immediate changes to seasonal factors lest it accidentally treats all changes as seasonal, which unfortunately means current estimates can suffer the most bias. Investigating historical precedents when there are big surprises often provides useful guidance about the amount and timing of any potential payback. Some judgement may also be needed to decide whether the news is noise or a sign of a different underlying inflation trend, which is what we ultimately want to reveal. Most models focus on broader macroeconomic variables, like wages, to understand how inflation should evolve over longer horizons.

3.2 The Phillips Curve

At the heart of most inflation forecasts is the so-called Phillips curve. Initially, at least, this was just postulating a negative relationship between inflation and unemployment. It then became a trade-off policymakers sought to exploit, and there was a breakdown in the relationship. More sophisticated variations are what persist today, typically focusing on wage inflation instead of price inflation to cut out the many noisy price-level shocks. Meanwhile, measures of spare capacity drive the inflationary pressure instead of simply unemployment. Inflation expectations are also potential drivers of the Phillips curve shifting. With so many moving parts, there are regular questions about the continued relevance of this approach. Poor specifications and unrealistic hopes for a linear curve are at least partly responsible for the critiques though.

3.2.1 Capacity Constraints

Unemployment works in the Phillips curve when it is a reasonable guide to the amount of spare productive capacity. Those people who are out of work will be more keenly incentivised to compete for work so unemployment should always be relevant. As people are individuals with personal abilities and interests, their competitiveness for new jobs will vary. A given unemployment rate does not always equate to the same level of inflation pressure. The matching efficiency of people with job openings matters. One popular way of discerning this matching in the labour market uses the Beveridge curve (named after another economist). This curve plots vacancy against unemployment rates over time. An outward shift in the curve means matching has worsened such that unemployment will be higher for any given level of vacancies.

By extracting parameters for the slope and intercept of Beveridge curves before and after a shock, it is possible to derive an implied change in the non-inflationary level of unemployment. Some straight best fit lines on an Excel chart is an easy way to do this. The gap between this and the actual unemployment rate provides a better measure of spare capacity because it allows for the non-inflationary level of inflation to vary over time. Terminology for this time-varying rate can be a bit confusing. References to the non-accelerating inflation rate of unemployment (NAIRU) don't help, as technically it is the wrong derivative. We're talking about something theoretically related to price acceleration and inflation changes (i.e. it should be "non-increasing"). Economists are not good at basic mathematics. Substituting wage for inflation in the name gives a mathematically correct acronym of NAWRU, which also matches its better use with wages rather than prices.

The natural unemployment rate is also often used interchangeably, though this is more of a long-term equilibrium concept. By definition, the NAWRU aims at the effective pressure on pay, and so it should be as variable as those underlying forces. It can be backed out from the observed data as such. A system of equations that define the fundamental relationships in the labour market first needs to be specified. A Phillips curve would be central to this. Then the statistically most likely values for the unemployment gap (unemployment rate less than the NAWRU) can be extracted for each point in time using the Kalman filter. Outcomes will be sensitive to the data, which are prone to revision, as well as the specification of the equations, so caution is needed when interpreting the results. As much as we crave conviction and point accuracy, that is not how this works. Ignoring the uncertainty and forming views on small differences could look inexplicably wrongheaded with the hindsight of revisions.

Developing a forward-looking view on the NAWRU itself, including where it might settle in the long term, requires an opinion on the structural drivers of unemployment. Changes in the tax and benefits system can cause changes in the incentives to work. Meanwhile, concentrated pockets of unemployment and financial problems can make it harder for potential workers to access available vacancies. Where this creates persistent pools of unemployment, skills will atrophy, and detachment from the labour market will grow. Persistent unemployment begets even more persistence. This effect is known as hysteresis, and it is a considerable concern to policymakers who prefer people productively working towards higher national living standards.

3.2.2 Slippery Slopes

Estimates of the unemployment gap can be plotted against wage growth to form a Phillips curve. Determining the inflationary influence requires the slope of the curve to be multiplied by the unemployment gap. That slope is the elasticity of wages to the unemployment gap, which is usually assumed to be constant in models. However, the data appear to suggest something else. When the unemployment gap is large, wage growth is not as weak as a linear relationship would suggest. This resilience may be because employees are relatively reluctant to take pay cuts, and employers are relatedly unwilling to impose them. Negative nominal wage growth has such a powerful psychological effect it is only worthwhile in extreme scenarios where the case is undeniable to all. There is in effect a nominal rigidity that bends the Phillips curve.

Some flattening of the Phillips curve may also reflect the variable competitiveness of the long-term unemployed. When unemployment is at a high cyclical rate, companies are spoilt for choice when hiring. Those who have been out of work for a long time will struggle to compete and have only a small effect on the pay bargaining. As unemployment falls, companies will find fewer candidates and higher pressure to pay up to secure them. The costs (including risk premium) of hiring the long-term unemployed person fall, and they have a bigger bearing on pay bargaining. An associated decline in the NAWRU slows the disappearance of the unemployment gap. Progress towards signs of a steeper portion of the Phillips curve can appear slow relative to unemployment's decline and add to the illusion that there is no curve. For those deceived by or deceiving with this illusion, a case for relatively stimulative policy can always be advanced, irrespective of the intellectual inconsistency.

Case study: fudging for looser policy

When unemployment is high, some economists will say that stimulus is needed to prevent hysteresis permanently harming potential as people lose the ability to compete. When unemployment is falling, the same economists argue that competition from the same people will weigh on inflation so need looser policy. Also hours or participation. Whatever justifies looser policy is fine until there is obvious inflation, and then it really isn't.

While the slope should always be sensitive to the level of the unemployment gap, there is an additional argument for the slope anyway having flattened over time. Reduced responsiveness of wage inflation to the unemployment gap is a sign of the stability that credibly independent monetary policymaking should bring. By not setting policy to the political cycle, unemployment is not driven as far below sustainable levels from which inflation follows. This stability means there is no exploration of the steepest portion of the Phillips curve, which makes the average for the recent period appear relatively flat. Moreover, in doing so, the extreme situations where inflation expectations start to shift have been avoided, thereby aiding their anchoring. To the extent that there is an actual flattening of the curve since the 1970s, it is probably mainly a function of this anchoring of inflation expectations.

3.2.3 Inflation Expectations

The role of inflation expectations here is something that gets taken for granted nowadays, but it was a late addition to this model. Indeed, it took the aggressive attempts of policymakers trying to exploit the relationship in the 1970s for the initial model to breakdown with runaway inflation. Fixing it saw the addition of a long-run vertical Phillips curve amid what could be multiple short-term curves. The short-term curves are the trade-off that policymakers were trying to exploit by pushing unemployment below the NAWRU, at the cost of an increase in inflation. Initially that inflationary policy came as a surprise to the public, but its repeated use stopped it from being so. Ultimately, expectations for a higher level of inflation merely became baked into pay settlements, and with wage costs higher, this pushed prices up too. This self-fulfilling feedback loop is a wage-price cycle.

An upward shift in the short-run Phillips curve could depict an increase in inflation expectations. It means that for any given level of the unemployment rate, nominal wage growth will be higher. And that wage growth will also be stronger relative to productivity, so this is a genuinely inflationary rise in unit wage costs. With a closed unemployment gap, wage inflation can prevail that is consistent with the rate of expected price inflation. Expectation effects introduce a fundamental uncertainty in the inflation outlook, and this requires nominally fixed contracts to price in an inflation risk premium. A simple workaround is to link the contracted price to realised inflation. Expectations are then explicitly adaptive. And they are also self-fulfilling when such inflation-linked contracts are in widespread use because of the cost pressure it exerts. Persistent price pressure after all cost shocks is the result, while the feedback loop means the inflationary effect is not a linear function of the initial shock unless inflation expectations are anchored.

The dynamics of inflation expectations matter considerably to the inflation outlook, yet for all the talk of them, there is no definitive observed data to use. Regular surveys of households and businesses can yield results systematically spread away from actual inflation. Most ordinary people do not even know what inflation is, and those who do are more likely to set their expectations around their current perceptions. Frequently purchased products like food and petrol play a larger role in such perceptions, so expectations also tend to change in response. Most people do not have the flexibility to include this inflationary view in their pay settlements, so there is not much relevance of the movements in these survey measures tracking current inflation. Financial market-based measures also arguably have little effect on real inflationary pressures. Real people and companies don't watch it, and market movements often have little to do with actual views of the inflation outlook (see Chap. 8).

It is the level of inflation expectations embedded in wages that we care about as it is this that affects costs and prices. The bad news is that this isn't observable. The good news is that the framework for backing out the similarly unobserved unemployment gap is extendable. Wage growth then becomes a function of the level of effective inflation expectations (no beta on this by definition), spare capacity and productivity. Those expectations might move adaptively and are thus loosely related to their previous values. The volatility of inflation may also positively contribute to changes in inflation as it raises uncertainty and justifies a risk premium. It is problematic in forecasts though because the prevalence of unforeseeable shocks should raise realised volatility above that of smoother model predictions. Attempts to predict volatility itself should suffer from less bias, but this volatility would not be consistent with wider estimates of the macromodel. Incorporating volatility into the model may not be worth it as a result, with useful historical estimates of effective inflation expectations possible to make either way.

Between nonlinearities and variable inflation expectations, it is feasible to place any observed combination of wage inflation and the unemployment gap on a Phillips curve. Measurement errors and transitory shocks need not be the primary reason for movements away from any previously stable curve. It is possible to back out what the statistically most likely mix is though. That does not mean it will be a perfect reflection of reality and revisions will affect it, but there continues to be more value in framing a forecast around the Phillips curve than not. It has earned its place at the heart of most macroeconomic models. Issues of the curve's slope, specification and expectations should not be forgotten though, to avoid leaning on the wrong curve.

3.3 Business Cycles

In Sect. 3.2, the effective unemployment gap was estimated using observed wage data. Taking GDP as given, this gap implies a potential level of GDP that might exist without inflationary pressure. Knowing how the potential level of output will evolve requires a more structural assessment. Between forecasts for this and actual GDP growth lies the output gap, which is strongly related to the unemployment gap but is broader in scope and of opposite sign (GDP = good; unemployment = bad). Different ways of doing this exist and can yield significantly different estimates and dynamics. In general, there is a bias for smooth changes in potential GDP, which causes significant changes in the output gap. And that relies on some dodgy assumptions. Relaxing them allows for more realistic complex dynamics. An advantage in forecasting the inflationary business cycle can emerge. Economic theory has surprisingly little to say about such cycles so beating it is admittedly a low bar.

3.3.1 Potential GDP

So far in this chapter, the emphasis has been on estimating the effective level of spare capacity before backing out where that leaves the level of potential GDP. Most economists do it the opposite way around, starting with a production function that uses the factors discussed in Chap. 2 and summing up potential GDP. Doing so leaves much less flexibility in potential GDP, thereby pushing large changes into the output gap, despite those factors not necessarily affecting inflation. More often than not, the choice of method seems to reflect the economists' bias. Forecasting power can be damned. A big output gap means a call for stimulative policy, which benefits bonds while raising equity price multiples for companies that anyway appear to have more room to grow. It, therefore, provides an excuse for investors to buy whatever the companies pitching such views are selling. If Goldman Sachs starts saying the opposite about the output gap, then there must be a massive bubble.

The production function style approach typically adds up data on capital, labour and estimates of total factor productivity (TFP). How to practically combine these factors of production is a key fundamental question. If there is a constant share of capital to labour over time, then a simple ratio is fine. Something like 70% labour and 30% capital can be assumed, with some TFP on top. This sort of specification is known as a Cobb–Douglas production function. An arguably less unrealistic alternative is to allow the labour/capital ratio to vary. Some assumed anchor is still needed and fixing the amount of additional capital required to replace an hour's labour (i.e. capital deepening) does that. This specification is a CES production function, which stands for the constant elasticity of substitution. With high transparency of assumption, that is what it says it is.

Total factor productivity is a particular problem in both production functions because it is unobservable. The usual derivation is to pass the residual of capital and labour against actual GDP through a Hodrick–Prescott filter, which is notoriously poor for such things. There are lots of fancy justifications for the TFP movements left afterwards, but it is essentially just there as a fudge factor for everything else, including structural changes. However, TFP can only capture structural changes with the benefit of considerable hindsight. Estimates soon after a break will completely miss it. A combination of extremely lagging data on capital and the smoothing effect of the filter means gaps are excessively persistent in the interim. Heavy bias on such occasions is the worst time for market views. In any case, adding up the factors of production in this way is to assume that they are equivalent and can thus either be applied elsewhere following a structural change or that there is no structural change. Neither assumption is realistic, but they are common in the economics profession.

Direct estimates of the margin of spare capacity can capture the effect of structural changes relatively rapidly. If some resources become obsolete as

GDP falls, they won't exert new disinflationary pressure, so direct estimates of disinflationary spare capacity won't increase, and the level of potential GDP correctly falls. These estimates of the output gap go much less negative in a recession, turn positive sooner but build smaller positive output gaps at cyclical peaks too. One retort is that these only guide to the margin of spare capacity in the short run, whereas idle resources elsewhere might come back on stream at a later date, thereby raising potential. There is some truth in this, but with an unknown proportion of idle resources becoming obsolete in the interim and not naturally transferable between sectors, it is easy to overstate such arguments. Because the idleness of resources is invisible, long-term idling arguments can prove spuriously persistent.

Case study: massively moving output gap estimates

Most estimates made before the Great Recession were for only a small positive output gap, consistent with inflation near the target. Then when GDP collapsed, the production function kept potential GDP up, pushing estimates towards saying that an enormous negative output gap had formed. As time went on, some of the hit became factored into potential GDP, but filters for total factor productivity naturally end up averaging out spare capacity over the crisis. This smoothing pushed up a big positive output gap pre-crisis and a much smaller one post-crisis, which was more consistent with inflation post-crisis but less so pre-crisis. Ideally, we would use something that works for both by allowing for more flexibility in potential GDP, which would be consistent with heterogeneous factors of production. Most models incorrectly assume the opposite—i.e. homogeneity through a single representative consumer—and that causes some crazy dynamics, including in how estimates evolve of the past.

While historical estimates can be backed out, clearly this cannot be possible in the forecast period where capacity is a crucial variable. Some structural assessments about the potential outlook for activity are needed. One of the easiest and arguably better ways of doing this is to use the NAWRU and labour force growth forecast to project potential employment growth. Then provided that there is no clear reason to assume there are significant cyclical capacity issues within firms, this can merely be multiplied by productivity to yield potential GDP growth. Changes in unemployment will then be translated into a change in inflationary pressures, while other stuff that is more ambiguous will have less impact on the forecast. Nor is this as gross a simplification as it might sound. If historical estimates of the unemployment gap assume it is the sole source of such disinflationary pressure, any capacity that might exist elsewhere will be lumped into the NAWRU anyway. The long-run level of the unemployment rate might be a bit off as a result, but potential GDP growth estimates need not be and that matters more for most markets.

3.3.2 Metastability

The additional volatility in potential GDP estimates that results from this simpler approach are both its strength and controversy. Most of this volatility comes from productivity shocks. If you adopt the conventional assumption that all people (factors of production generally) are the same, then there shouldn't be much volatility. Relocating resources do not change how productive they are in that model. This assumption also removes the role of the entrepreneur in finding efficiencies and leaves productivity growth as being almost a mythical thing that just happens. That doesn't sound right, and the data don't back it up. Breaks periodically punctuate stability in productivity trends. Those breaks naturally coincide with large shocks. When the economy rebalances, resources need to move, and there is a mixture of obsolescence and under-utilisation in the process. At the end of it, resources are in areas that may have a different underlying rate of return, and so the new productivity trend can be distinct from the last.

Dynamics of the productivity data can be seen to resemble a moving average of growth marked by discontinuities rather than mainstream theory's average. In more mathematical terms, the observed equilibrium appears to be metastable, not a steady state. Allowing flexibility in productivity, as anyway seems to exist in the data of most countries, creates a similarly metastable equilibrium. Matching the type of displayed dynamics should be a prerequisite for a model, but a mainstream focus on comparing theoretical steady states (so-called comparative statics) means it barely registers as an afterthought. There are complications of modelling things this way, not least because the outlook is more dependent on the path it is following. Such path dependence means simple rules of thumb about the response of the economy to some shocks require recalibration in different states of the world. Something that seems small may still trigger an enormous economic change. Ignoring this uncertainty does not prevent it existing in a real market economy, but it does prevent planning for it.

Real people do not act in the collectively rational ways of mainstream models because they are self-interested individuals without perfect insight. With expectations often adapted based on realised outcomes, self-fulfilling confidence cycles can emerge. House prices are a classic example of this (see case study). When something is a function of itself, nonlinear dynamics follow, and large economic imbalances can rationally accumulate. Such imbalances can build quicker and persist for longer than might seem reasonable at the time because it is essentially a self-sustained equilibrium. When the imbalances correct, the process can also be more abrupt and go further, not least because by that time there will likely be lots of explanations as to why bubbly behaviour can be justified. Markets make opinions. And the simplest ideas sell best, even if they miss the point, like the metastability here.

3.3.3 Neutral Interest Rates

It is real phenomena that comprise the economic cycle, but it is monetary factors that arguably cause the cycle. For those who view policymakers as benign guides of the economy back to equilibrium, there may be a vigorous dispute of this caricature. However, the favourable view rests heavily on the hope that the allocation of resources does not matter. More activity now is merely better. In the real world, resource allocations determine the return on them. Such an unrealistic mainstream assumption means we should be circumspect about attempts to manipulate the distribution of resources because stimulus can also carry costs. Nor is this just an issue of asset misallocation because the level, price and distribution of debt and equity are also affected. Together this affects the affordability and sustainability of balance sheets and the outlook for activity by extension.

Austrian business cycle theory formalises the role of policy in driving the cycle. It sees the seeds of a crisis planted in the stimulus that preceded it. Intuitively, risks have to accumulate before they can correct. When interest rates are below the level consistent with prevailing preferences for current consumption and investment, there is an unsustainable encouragement to front-load spending. Investment projects motivated by new found demand and made viable by low-interest rates are thereby riskily built on unsound foundations. A normalisation of rates will reveal the malinvestments and cause a correction in the economy that could be quite painful. Policymakers may drive adjustment by raising rates in response to some resultant inflationary pressure, or the shock could come from the real economy itself. Once someone has used their balance sheet for acquisition, they are in a weaker position to do so again. Future demand growth is thereby fundamentally reduced after an early spending spree. Failure to force the necessary correction is a recipe for straddling the economy with more debt and less real savings to be properly invested, condemning the economy to a slower trend. One way or another, the fundamental problems of past malinvestments will reveal themselves.

The revelation of imbalances as the economy tips over into recession can be called a (Hyman) Minsky moment, after the post-Keynesian economist. There are similarities to the Austrian business cycle theory at this stage of the cycle too. However, they have opposing views on whether policy interventions help or hinder in the long run. Agreement that monetary policy can be stimulative in the short term means the monetary policy setting matters either way. The deviation of interest rates from an estimate of the neutral rate ("r star") denotes the amount of stimulus or tightening. By definition, when rates are at their neutral setting, the economy will grow at its potential pace. This neutrality makes it possible to back out the effective policy environment and the neutral rate by extension from changes in the economy's spare capacity, which is itself an unobserved quantum. In both cases, statistical techniques like the Kalman filter need to be used to find the most likely value for what the unobserved variables are.

Numerous structural factors persistently affect the level of the neutral interest rate over time. They do this by shifting the balance of savings and investment. So demographic factors influence this because people save up for their retirement when those savings start to be spent, which would put downward and then upward pressure on the neutral rate. Upward pressure could also come from a cheapening of capital goods prices as this would encourage investment. More controversial is the downward effect arising from inequality where the wealthy have a lower marginal propensity to consume. To the extent that there is an appropriate investment of those savings, they might raise productivity growth and the neutral interest rate instead. As ever, the efficient allocation of resources matters, not just the fact that there has been an allocation somewhere.

Cyclical factors can also affect this and not just from the domestic economy. Foreign trading partners will have economic cycles that may not always align. When one strengthens (or weakens) the natural return on assets, there will have risen (or fallen), causing its exchange rate to appreciate (or depreciate). That compounds the rise (or fall) in demand for imports to the benefit (or loss) of countries exporting to it. This then puts some upward (or downward) pressure on the neutral rate in the exporters' country. Moreover, to the extent a loose (or tight) fiscal policy is raising the natural rate of return on an investment; the neutral rate will be raised (or lowered) for a time. Again, the allocation of resources related to those fiscal policies matters so there can be payback as the rate of return converges back to underlying realities.

Taken from the other perspective, it is the consistency with time preferences of consumers that matter for ultimate sustainability. For any given natural rate of return on their resources, households will have a preference for earning it and consuming in the future versus spending in the present. So a higher neutral rate is an encouragement to defer demand, while a lower neutral rate encourages spending now. If there is a manipulation of interest rates away from this neutral level, an undesired level of real savings will occur. The future level and composition of real resources will then differ from previously desired levels, potentially creating a new neutral rate.

Feedback between the policy setting and the future neutral rate is not a feature of mainstream models. Potential output growth is considered broadly independent of monetary policy and is relatively stable. That is partly because of the assumed irrelevance of resource allocations. If people had perfect collective foresight, as assumed, this would prevent policies from fooling them. Whereas in practice, it is rational for individuals to participate in a boom, artificial or otherwise, in the hope of collecting a personal profit and getting out ahead of the herd. Hope that policymakers with benevolent intentions have a benign economic effect is arguably another factor contributing to the sorry state of economics. It helps here that the state funds so much of the deep research assuming that.

Whatever their merits, policy interventions are an unavoidable aspect of the real economy, and they have real market effects. With the underlying economic framework constructed, it is time to bring the policymakers more into the mix. Bring on Part 2.

Main Messages

- Inflation is a rise in prices. At its most general, this can be thought of as an increase in the money supply, as was classically the case. With more money, the purchasing power of each unit reduces so more money is needed to buy something. Where the money goes, prices will rise, rather than it being uniform.
- Changes in the price of consumer goods and services are the common usage of "inflation", but this is only one place money may go. Artificially inflated prices elsewhere still carry costs and can cause considerable structural instabilities in the economy.
- Measuring inflation is not a trivial task. Price aggregation is needed but tastes change over time and are unknown at the most detailed level. The combination process introduces bias, with a political preference to the downside.

- Forecasting consumer price inflation requires knowledge of pricing behaviour and cost pressures in particular. Unit wage costs are an apparent underlying source of inflation. Spare capacity depresses this, as embodied by the Phillips curve.
- Capacity constraints cannot be directly recorded. However, statistical techniques can be used to back out the most likely level of effective spare capacity consistent with observed data.
- There are some signs of a flattening of the Phillips curve, meaning spare capacity has less effect on inflation. Some of this may be because large amounts of slack have less impact amid aversion to below zero real and especially nominal pay growth.
- With contemporary policymakers preventing significant capacity constraints, inflation expectations have not been encouraged to spiral higher, which would be an effective outward shift in the Phillips curve that also appears like a very steep portion of it.
- The potential level of GDP consistent with non-excessive inflation can be backed out from estimates of spare capacity or summed up from estimates and assumptions about the underlying factors of production. The latter is less flexible and cannot catch structural changes in anything approaching a useful timeframe.
- In reality, the structure of the economy is constantly evolving. As resources move, they can become underemployed or obsolete, with this creating breaks in productivity trends. Where resources end up determines their new return. Such dynamics are of a metastable equilibrium, not the standard steady state one.
- When spare capacity is being used up, the monetary policy setting is stimulative, with rates below their neutral setting. Structurally, saving and investment determine that neutral rate, which in turn reflect the natural expected return on investment and time preferences.

Further Reading

Ball, Philip. 2005. Critical Mass: How One Thing Leads to Another. Arrow.

Friedman, Milton. 1971. *A Monetary History of the United States 1867–1960.* Princeton University Press.

Gleik, James. 1997. *Chaos: Making a New Science*. Vintage.

Minsky, Hyman. 2008. *Stabilising an Unstable Economy*. McGraw Hill Professional.

Office for National Statistics. 2014. *Consumer Price Indices: Technical Manual.*

www.mises.org.

Part II

Stabilisers

Dynamics of the real economy were built upon theoretical foundations in Part 1. An appreciation for some of the central relationships is needed to anticipate and track developments in them. However, the economy is not evolving in a vacuum. Policymakers will also assess what is going on in the economy and use the tools they have available to make things better. Whether they achieve that or not is another matter, but the actions of policymakers cannot be ignored. Having a great call on the economy and the financial market implications of that is not enough if a surprise intervention overrides both. After all, counterfactuals don't trade; reality does, across all the probability-weighted potential outlooks. A coherent call on the market will incorporate the reaction function of policymakers and consider trades in that response as well as the net economic effect of everything. The ultimate effect and the intent might not match, but that is merely another opportunity for investors.

The most direct form of intervention comes from fiscal policymakers. Subject to constitutional restrictions, the people setting the sovereign laws of their nation can pretty much make whatever targeted interventions they like. Rigging prices, controlling volumes or using taxes are all the preserve of fiscal policymakers. Meanwhile, monetary policymakers are typically independent nowadays and lack the democratic legitimacy to intervene too directly into people's lives, although that doesn't mean monetary policy has no effect. On the contrary, monetary policy has become the primary tool for demand management in most countries, but it is a relatively indiscriminate tool able to meet limited objectives. Forward guidance on the economy and the expected monetary policy response to that is useful and can have significant effects by itself. With limited long-run effects of monetary policy and more structural imbalances to consider, macroprudential policies have gained prominence as a third toolkit since the Great Recession. These seek to trim tail risks and tame the cycle while leaving monetary policy to focus on its mandate. That inevitably intrudes in more targeted ways, so policymakers are treading more carefully, but it is an important part of the overall stabilisation toolkit. This part will, in turn, explore the details of deploying fiscal, monetary and macroprudential policies.

4
Fiscal Policy

Governments have significant powers to intervene in their economies. It is only political and constitutional constraints that bind them domestically as the government can rewrite restrictive laws. Political factors change over time, and if the government wants to do something, it only needs to see support for it on one occasion to pass it. That "one-touch" hurdle is easier to clear, which could be crucial if amendments are to more fundamental legal limitations. This chapter will begin with a discussion of the main types of interventions in the economy and what effect they have. Following that are policies to more broadly stabilise the economy, scenarios for how the state's balance sheet might constrain the response and the sort of international support available to get a government out of a hole.

4.1 Market Interventions

There is no shortage of ways that a government can intervene in markets if it so desires. When things are not working as well as hoped, there is pressure to do something about it. Capping prices, rationing, wage controls, taxes or subsidies can all seem like natural ways of appeasing an electorate. Doing so can bring political advantage, at least in the short term. Interventions carry costs that some politicians might not anticipate. Correcting for the costs of previous interventions can be an excuse to do more. Some politicians may even ideologically seek this from the start, while others just prefer to pass

P. Rush, *Real Market Economics*,
https://doi.org/10.1057/978-1-349-95278-6_4

the blame rather than taking responsibility. It can be a dangerous path that is much easier to join than to leave. An understanding of how interventions interact with incentives will at least prepare you for the consequences.

4.1.1 Setting Hard Limits

At the blunter end of the policy toolkit is the setting of hard limits on prices or quantities. These were especially popular in the style of socialism that prevailed during the 1970s when more governments still had nationalised control over many industries. Controls can nonetheless be levied on private companies too and doing so is a viable way of signalling virtuous sympathy with the peoples' cost of living. Utilities are particularly susceptible to such demands because consumption is widespread and few substitutes exist. When prices are rising, or at least the financial burden is amid a real income reduction, consumers have to spend a higher proportion of their incomes on such necessities. By squeezing out welfare-enhancing discretionary purchases, consumers feel worse off and can demand something is done about the situation. Price controls can be a natural reflex.

Under normal circumstances, companies' supply curves are upward sloping. At a higher price level, they can afford to produce more before diseconomies of scale cause the marginal cost of doing so to exceed the marginal revenue again. By intervening to set a lower price, some proportion of that output ceases to be profitable, and volumes can fall accordingly. Producers still lose out from the cap as they are now selling less at a lower price. Consumers will also lose out, though, because there are people who would like to have consumed some output that now can't because producers aren't allowed to sell it to them at a profitable price, despite the willingness to buy. Overall, Fig. 4.1 illustrates the deadweight loss from the cap.

There might be a temptation to say that developed countries have plenty of potential supply in all the utilities, and customers are not going to face reduced availability. It nonetheless remains a question of degree. A short-lived price cap that leaves companies unable to cover their fixed costs in the short term is temporarily tolerable, but those costs ultimately need to be covered so if the cap is too low, firms will leave the market. Different cost structures between companies can cause smaller ones to leave earlier and competition to be constrained to the degree that prices might ultimately end up higher than without the cap, but output still constrained. Hosepipe bans in summers or subsidies to stop industrial firms producing during peak energy demand are examples of the sort of shortages that arise from price interventions.

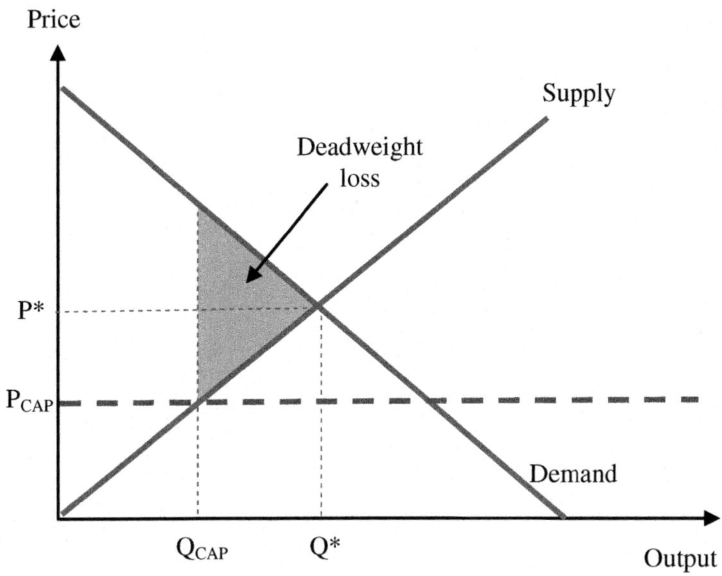

Fig. 4.1 Price cap deadweight loss

The need for companies to reduce output in such circumstances can also arise from restrictions on demand elsewhere. In this energy example, the producer might be pressured to generate using renewable energy sources that are more expensive, which encourages the price cap by extension. Those renewables are also typically unreliable sources of power and can't be guaranteed to deliver it when required. Maintaining spare generation capacity is also expensive and won't happen at low prices, so rationing of supply to some volunteers can be the only way to avoid involuntary general brownouts and blackouts. Volunteers would have to be paid back at a price level commensurate with their demand at this more limited level of availability, and with a typically downward sloping demand curve, that price could be far higher (Fig. 4.2). Producers lose money when implementing such restrictions, but such rationing may remain rational if it is cheaper than alternativity maintaining spare generation capacity.

A less usual class of control is the minimum price, which might exist in the above example as a floor on the price of carbon, or on other things with negative side effects that the government wants to discourage, like alcohol. By far the most common form of minimum price, though, is for the price of labour. There is an odd equivalence here—minimum prices are used to prevent the output of bad things, but also employment, which is considered a good thing. For clarity, a minimum wage is a ban on certain jobs. To the

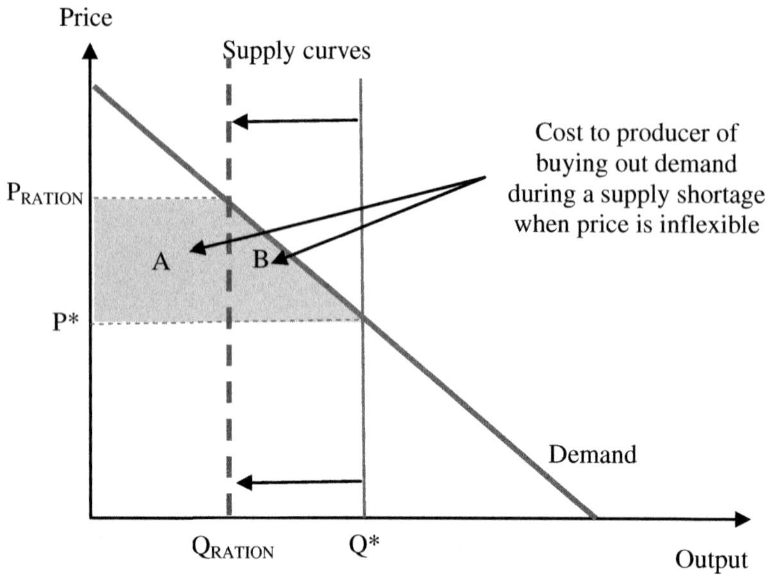

Fig. 4.2 Cost of rationing

extent that this ban prevents people from working at a wage rate both they and their employer are otherwise happy with, unemployment can be created (Fig. 4.3).

Calling the minimum wage, a job ban wouldn't be a brilliant way of branding a policy sold to workers as being in their interests, but it is what it is. The idea behind this policy is that employees are exploited, and by setting a minimum wage, they will gain a degree of protection. Without the ability to exploit the lowest paid workers, companies will choose to pay higher salaries, which would still be profitable for them to do. Introductions of minimum wages have not typically caused an apparent surge in unemployment, which has emboldened calls to expand such policies into higher wage rates. However, where the minimum wage is high relative to average earnings, problems arise. A higher relative minimum wage will capture more of the workforce and not in a linear way under a typical income distribution. A small rise can have no effect when the floor is low but a huge effect when it is high.

There is no exploitation of all workers to a significant degree, and exploitation itself can be a relative thing. A top-up payment for workers to reach the minimum wage may be extracted from other employees when the lowest paid portion lacks value in isolation but is necessary to what everyone else does for the business. A higher minimum wage means there are fewer

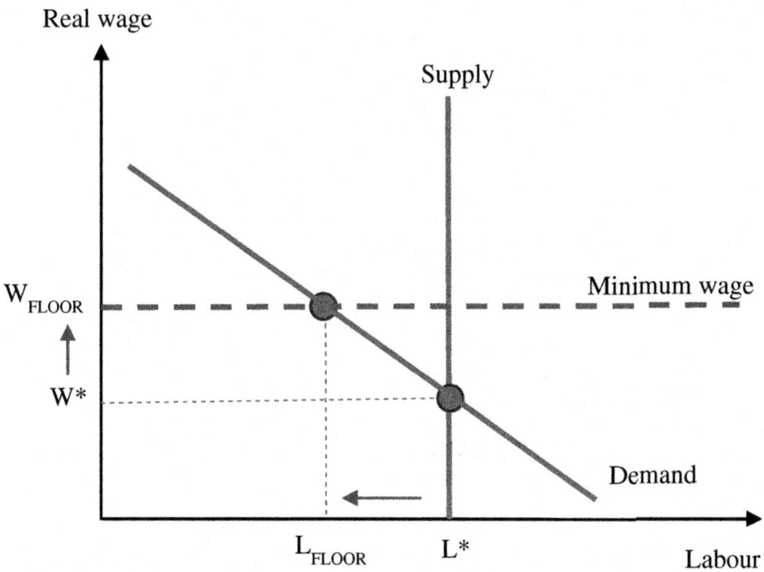

Fig. 4.3 Minimum wages

workers left available for exploitation in the name of subsidising the lowest paid, which also harms their work incentives when such transfers occur. When competitors are facing similar wage pressures, the business might be able to raise its prices to pay its growing wage bill. Otherwise, like when the company competes in export markets, the cost of business may become prohibitive, and it could choose to leave the market. Weaker output and employment are the natural effect of minimum wages, albeit with the effect only becoming evident when higher rates capture a larger share of the workforce.

4.1.2 Taxes and Subsidies

Rather than drawing a hard line in price or volume terms, the government can also choose to intervene in a slightly more subtle way by introducing taxes or subsidies. Either could potentially hit production itself or the various factors used in the process. Doing so can be desirable when there are externalities from production decisions that are not factored into the price and level of output otherwise. Introducing the tax or benefit internalises that cost for the business and forces it to be taken into account, as illustrated in Fig. 4.4.

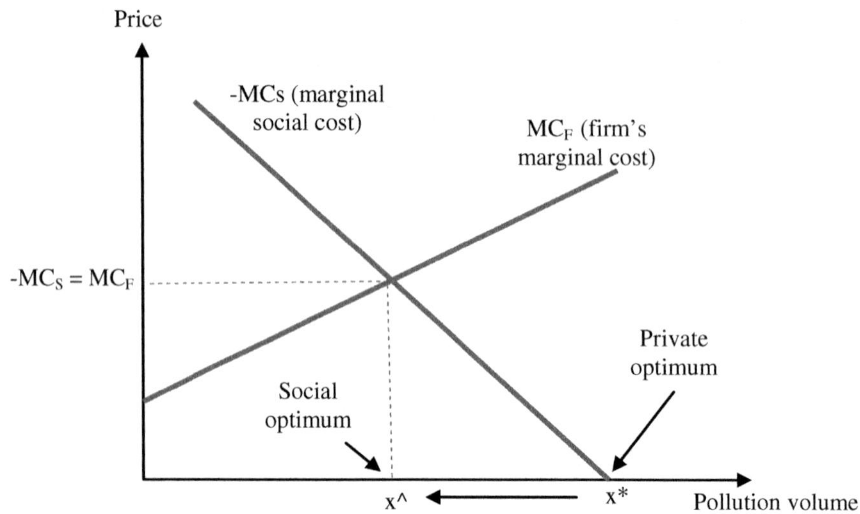

Fig. 4.4 Social costs

So subsidies of agricultural output might occur because society benefits from food security and a well-maintained natural environment. On the other side, taxation of alcohol and tobacco might occur because of the adverse effects on health and society.

In practice, it is not entirely straightforward how to do this. It is not just a case of knowing how to calculate the cost to society of various things, but also about where to draw the line. Sometimes, the latter has such a large effect it determines the sign of the net cost. For example, smoking harms health. Those passively smoking suffer for something they did not choose to do, which is one externality. Smokers are also more likely to suffer from health issues that are very costly to treat, and the smoker should arguably be made to pay for that too. Focusing on these factors justifies very high tobacco tax rates. However, because of those same health issues, longevity is significantly reduced and that saves on the expense of pensions, social care and treating longer-term health problems. Once this factor is taken into account too, the overall cost to society of smoking could be negative instead, depending on the national system. That could justify subsidising people to smoke and die off quickly. Whether such signals are morally or politically reasonable to send provides an anchor on where to draw the defining line, but none of this is going to be something set in stone.

The cut-off for what social costs to tax is never going to identify areas able to raise enough money to pay for all the things that government wants to buy. Most revenue raising is because the government believes it can deploy some of its citizens' money better than they can. Similar to the above examples, there are legitimate occasions when a collective payment by the government on behalf of its people is socially optimal. Such scenarios might arise from a desire among citizens to free ride on others expense, like enjoying the collective security of defence and the domestic rule of law or the reduced health risks from vaccinating others. There might also be instances of natural monopolies where money can be raised, levying a charge on the extraction of raw materials from the state's oceans or selling radio spectrum.

Most taxation and government spending are not as clear cut as any of these things. There is instead a set of time-varying social norms that politicians position themselves within. Much of this falls within a broadly defined category of redistributive policy. Redistributions are the direct transfer of money, typically towards poorer people so that they can avoid destitution. At a basic level, this reflects some simple human compassion, but it also leaves recipients of support with a better platform to withstand adverse shocks and return to productive lives. An industrious future is in everyone's economic interests. The sale of universal education and health care can sometimes similarly be sold as ways to maximise everyone's potential. However, there is a point at which such things are taken too far. With each increase in taxation, there is upward pressure on prices and an incentive to reduce output, with the private sector losing out by more than just the value of the tax (Fig. 4.5). And on the other side, too much state support impedes work incentives, which is something policymakers must be mindful of when designing systems for stabilising the economy.

4.2 Fiscal Stabilisers

As much as policymakers might wish away recessions, they are an unavoidable economic reality. Declaring an end to boom and bust, as former UK Chancellor of the Exchequer Gordon Brown famously did, does not make it so. It merely means you are poorly prepared for a downturn when it inevitably occurs. There are nonetheless some fiscal levers that engage automatically in a slowdown. Beyond that is the discretionary delivery of active policy measures. All, of course, are subject to sustainability restrictions, which is the subject of the section after this one.

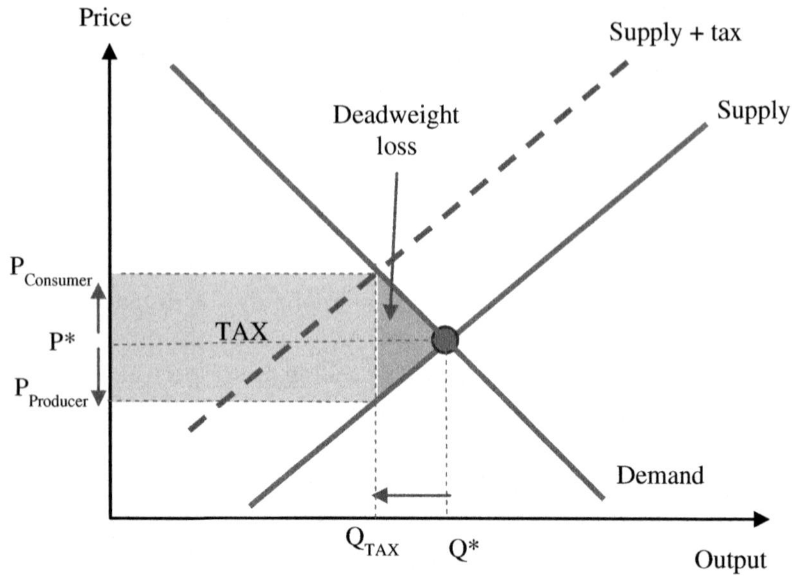

Fig. 4.5 Taxation's deadweight loss

4.2.1 Automatic Stabilisers

Most governments have a social security system. Some level of that is designed to support those with disabilities that cannot work. Such claims should be broadly immune to fluctuations in the economic cycle, although there often is some cyclicality to them. Disabilities do not come in black and white. Through the colourful spectrum in between, many people may find their employment options limited to some degree by their disability, but who would prefer to work if possible. When out of work, they might be eligible to claim benefits as a disabled person, which are typically at a relatively high level, and that inevitably introduces some cyclicality.

Many countries also offer some state support for anyone out of work, subject to some conditionality. Voluntarily leaving work or turning down work might invalidate such claims, for example. Sometimes, the benefit has an explicitly contributory aspect to it. Whatever the rules, the existence of such benefits provides a safety net for people losing their jobs. When the economic cycle turns down, and employees become redundant, these benefits automatically kick in for more people. Receipt of these benefits provides money that claimants can use to minimise contractions in their consumption. The existence of such benefits thereby automatically provides some fiscal stimulus at a time when it is needed to stabilise the economy—hence the term "automatic stabilisers".

The tax system was also designed to help it smooth out the cycle. The most tax levied comes from the flow of activity rather than the stock. That means taxing wages, sales, profits and dividends more than the stock of wealth. By doing it this way, a slowdown in the economy causes the same for the taxable flow of activity. The government in effect shares in the successes and stresses of its citizens. Taxing wealth or other things that do not vary with the economic cycle are, in contrast, burdens that leave people less able to withstand adverse shocks when they occur. The reduction in revenues that occurs from the traditional taxation sources is the other primary sort of automatic stabiliser in the economy. Amid uncertainty in the current state of the economy, let alone the future state, and the lags involved in politicians announcing changes in fiscal policy, such stabilising tools are valuable.

4.2.2 Active Stimulus

Having some stimulus that kicks in automatically is desirable, but it is not always enough, especially when the public exerts political pressure for something to be done. As former US Treasury Secretary said during the global credit crunch: "plan beats no plan". The existence of a plan can help shore up confidence (and votes) and encourage consumers and businesses to continue spending rather than precautionarily retrench. Additional government expenditure can itself more directly motivate private sector spending. The public investment might open up new opportunities for businesses, and together with consumption, spending should keep more people employed and able to spend themselves.

Overstating the merits of active stimulus measures is easy. Politicians rarely struggle to spend money when it's sloshing around, and they tend to treat it as a slush fund for their political projects. So-called pork barrel politics leads to projects with very low economic returns. That's a problem because ultimately, taxpayers will have to pay for whatever the government is spending. An opportunity cost comes from what the private sector could have done with that money instead. Some people say that even paying people to dig and fill holes back in is worthwhile, but this is a nonsensically myopic view. Doing something with no productive return whatsoever is a waste that will weigh on the economy's future growth when it becomes time to pay for it, assuming that the market is even willing to finance such a frivolous fiscal deficit.

At the theoretical extreme lies so-called Ricardian equivalence. This hypothesis is that people will anticipate the future burden of taxation to pay for current fiscal stimulus and reduce their current expenditure accordingly.

To the extent that this is true, the stimulus would not even serve to support the economy in the short term. It would merely cause a substitution between private-sector spending and public-sector spending in the near term, with an unwind later. In practice, people are not able to perfectly see the future and even when they realise taxes may rise in future, that doesn't dissuade them from enjoying higher spending in the short term. It is, after all, rational to prefer good things now rather than later. A lot could also happen to reduce the burden of future taxation, including growth in real incomes.

Away from the extremes, all fiscal policies are still not the same. Different types of expenditure will support the economy in various ways and to varying degrees. For example, investment in the capital stock will raise the productive potential of the economy and tends to be more valuable than government consumption. As with private investment, different projects will have differing rates of return on them. In other words, the multiplier effect of that expenditure on the economy will also vary. The same goes for tax cuts. Households and businesses have different propensities to consume the extra money made available by tax cuts. All such things can also be state dependent. For example, if the housing market is weak, reducing transaction taxes might be more powerful than otherwise. It would also better align with the political pressures that probably prevail in such a scenario. That is why discretion over what discretionary fiscal stimulus measures to use is needed, and the outcome delivered can't be determined well ahead of the negative shock itself. Rather than get too bogged down in political judgements, many independent forecasts, including central banks, will assume that changes in government spending score on GDP one for one, while politicians are naturally minded to use far higher multipliers.

Stimulus doesn't have to be overt and directly interventionist. Sometimes, it is enough to shield the private sector from the tail risk and leave it to allocate the resources. As the private sector tends to be far more efficient and should have a pipeline of projects under consideration, such guarantees can be powerful. There can be a lot to like politically too. A guarantee doesn't cost anything up front and might even raise revenue as a sale of an option. If the risk crystallises and the option triggered, the government might be on the hook for a lot of money, but until then, it can potentially enjoy stimulus without having to raise any cash. Moreover, such contingent liabilities don't store in conventional fiscal measures. That doesn't mean the risks disappear of course. When the economy turns down, these exposures come on to the government balance sheet and risk scaring investors about sustainability.

4.3 Sustainability

In normal times, the sustainability of government interventions is determined by political factors. People like having personal and economic freedoms. Take too much away, and they will be minded to vote for change, or where that option doesn't exist, potentially rise and overthrow their rulers. There is, of course, a higher hurdle to doing the latter than the former, but the threshold for change can anyway vary beyond underlying local social preferences. If the failings of past interventions are blameable on other things, propaganda might be able to sustain or even extend the government's reach. But with growth typically slower and happiness reduced as the size of the state's intrusions rise, at some stage, change will come. International support in such circumstances is controversial. Contingent support may be forthcoming when the problem is one of finance rather than democratic legitimacy, but that is broadly a separate issue.

4.3.1 Political Sustainability

At least in the short term, opinion polls provide a guide as to whether the threshold for change is close to being cleared. Governments will similarly be watching such surveys while also conducting private meetings with focus groups. Neither can ever be 100% reliable. Attempts must be made to align the sample groups with the targeted population, but what characteristics to align and how to weight respondents' propensity to cast votes make an enormous difference. There is also an inherent conflict of interest. When political polls send a strong message, it raises the demand for commissioning more polls, so there is a clear incentive to fiddle the parameters beyond reasonable attempts to calibrate the survey. Sometimes, measures of economic performance can provide a more reliable guide to voting habits than the opinion polls. Picking the right measures to reflect the relevant population's mood makes this a fraught task that is more usually better suited to explain why people voted the way they did rather than anticipating it.

Over longer horizons, a better way of predicting political trends is to look for where the dominant political vacuum is. Good politics for an election frequently involves triangulating one's position between the party's traditional base and the opposition. This strategy helps stake a claim to the centre ground where most votes are harvested. It is worth considering multiple triangulation scenarios. A single one can be quickly upended by an unknown factor, while multiple ones prepare for shocks that might shift what outcome seems to be the single most likely. International commentators often like to draw themes together from recent results and assume that the same will be relevant elsewhere. Different electoral systems determine the impact of any given swing, though. And more often than not, the domestic idiosyncrasies are far more pertinent to voters than whatever the international factor is in the debate. It is the job of the chattering classes to opine on such things, just try not to mistake an interesting explanation of the past for an ability to forecast the future.

4.3.2 Fiscal Sustainability

Over the typical market relevant horizons, fiscal factors determine how market participants view the sustainability of the government's plans. The ultimate arbiter is always whether the government can raise enough money. Most of this revenue is coming from domestic taxpayers, hence the relevance of political sustainability, but this source is less likely to trigger a financing problem. Small sizes of individual contributions and a lack of coordination make it difficult to exert power this way. Nor is it necessarily desirable to cause a financial crisis where you live and probably have the bulk of your assets. If fiscal plans are looking unsustainable, it is likely to be financial market participants who force the matter instead.

International lenders have other options of places to invest their portfolios. Concerns about the fiscal trajectory would require compensation with higher interest rates, which will at least make it more expensive for the government to borrow. Given the large stock of debt that countries have to refinance periodically, along with the flow of borrowing that a profligate state probably has, this interest rate rise can leave the government with no choice but to change policy. Failure to do so will rapidly deteriorate the fiscal metrics that matter and eventually lead to a loss of market access where all spending will need to be covered by domestic taxes. Such aggressive actions by so-called bond vigilantes are forecast more frequently than occurs, though. Investing in global government bonds is partly a relative thing, which a widespread shock does not affect much. Extensive pressure is also needed, lest the government be left able to parry the attack at an extreme cost to the portfolio. And the rise of passive investing puts more weight on a group of investors who will never lead such an attack, even if they might be pulled into one by market movements once one begins.

There is a broad range of measures that activist investors will be watching to gauge fiscal sustainability. Most will be highly related to each other in definition and trends. Broadly speaking, they are either flow or mainly stock measures. On the flow side, that means the amount of borrowing, both regarding the cash requirement and the rate at which obligations accrue. Sometimes, debt interest payments will be stripped out to yield the so-called primary balance. All are about the fiscal deficit and for comparisons between countries, and they are usually stated as a share of GDP. Indicators on the stock side relate to the level of overall debt. Ideally, this should incorporate off-balance sheet commitments as an additional cross-check on the fiscal position, although such data are of variable quality. GDP is once again a useful equaliser for comparisons, but tax revenues are also a good comparator to use. Very long-term forecasts for both the flow and stock variables also provide guidance as to how sustainability is affected by demographic changes, which is useful information even though such numbers shall certainly be wrong.

One of the most significant adjustments to make is also one of the most difficult. It involves adjusting borrowing numbers for the effects of the economic cycle. When output has fallen below an economy's potential, growth can occur without generating excessive inflation, but raising tax revenues and reducing benefit expenditures all the same. Temporary shortfalls in demand increase borrowing in the short term, but it is less of a problem when the economy has room to grow out of the problem. The real burden comes when the productive potential of the economy also suffers. When that is the cause of demand weakness, the fiscal deficit will not disappear of its own accord because there is no cyclical recovery on the horizon. In such circumstances, the government must implement fiscal consolidation measures to fill the hole. Estimating the economy's position in the economic cycle is, therefore, an important factor for active market participants. Some caution is still needed as a different calibration of automatic stabilisers to GDP means that different adjustment processes may be necessary. The rough rule of thumb is just to subtract the output gap from the fiscal deficit, though.

It is increasingly popular to appoint independent forecasters as a way to lend greater credibility to all of these fiscal forecasts. Ignorance might be bliss in the short term, but it is better to know the extent of any problems rather than fear they may be far bigger. Together with a credible set of fiscal targets, independence reduces uncertainty in the outlook, and thus the risk premium markets demand as compensation for lending to the government. By extension, there should be more tolerance among market participants to finance the government in future. It is a direct parallel to the logic behind independent central banks, which are discussed in the next chapter, although they are far more common. When both have a quasi-autonomous relationship with the government, a coordination issue may arise from the difficulty of the fiscal agent to publish forecasts that contradict the central bank.

If the fiscal forecaster believes that the economy is in a more advanced stage of the economic cycle than the central bank does, it will forecast additional inflationary pressures. For a central bank targeting that, or implicitly activity, and claiming that it is doing everything necessary to meet its goal, the inconsistency could appear as an accusation that the central bank isn't doing its job. There is a temptation to fudge the forecast to say the other is doing its job fine, but this is not costless to fiscal policy. Raising the assumed margin of spare capacity in the economy means that the structural budget deficit is smaller than it otherwise would be. And with more room for the economy to grow, forecasts would show a quicker fall in the deficit and less need for discretionary fiscal tightening. That's great if the adopted view of the central bank is correct, but it's potentially problematic if the fiscal authority was closer to the truth instead. The fiscal problem would then be bigger than assumed, and with the economic cycle at a more advanced stage, the risk of a recession would be larger. That's a toxic combination: weaker public finances at a time when they should be strong. The long-term economic costs of erring towards extreme prudence are probably less than for leaving a deficit that is too large, but the reverse cost split is arguably right at a political level. The latter often prevails, even when it is against prevailing rhetoric, as was the case in the UK after the Great Recession.

Case study—UK fiscal austerity after the recession

The UK economy was not prepared for the Great Recession, as its large finance industry had been used to provide revenues for government largesse elsewhere over many years. When imbalances started to correct, an enormous structural fiscal deficit opened up, and the government eventually needed to do something. Rhetoric was primarily of prudent fiscal austerity, but the reality remained far more profligate. When a forecast suggested more fiscal room, there was more spending, while reduced room caused targets to be amended. The political cost of the necessary measures to defend a target was too high. The UK government liked to metaphorically blame Labour for "failing to mend the roof while the sun was shining", which meant fixing the finances in the rain. By extension, the political reaction function caused the builders' tea breaks to be far too frequent and progress painfully slow. Some tacked on roofing felt and an "under construction" sign are a weak defence against the next storm. But the prudent rhetoric was tolerated because the opposition party's building crew did not look like they even wanted to build a roof, which removed the competitive pressure to deliver fiscal consolidation.

4.3.3 International Bailout

Fiscal largesse can become so excessive that market pressures demand consolidation at a very painful pace. The government could essentially lose the ability to deliver cuts in the areas that minimise the economic cost, and over a period that the general public can adapt to. Instead, the government must cut whatever it can as quickly as possible. Cancelling investment projects is often an easy victim, despite the high cost to future productive potential. Cuts to government salaries can be another target, even though shocking real incomes so directly can cause a similarly panicked response from the private sector that deepens recessionary tendencies. Some economists argue that the costs of consolidation can be so high as to counteract the savings themselves. That's probably only true at the most extreme pace. Nonetheless, there is a realistic point that there is an optimal pace of consolidation to consider, which is likely to be somewhat slower than the market can require but also faster than will be argued for by either those dependent on the state or the many academics who are always biased towards big governments.

If a government finds itself in this awkward position, pressured by markets to deliver fiscal consolidation at a suboptimally fast pace, there is a case to seek support from elsewhere. Support might come through a bilateral or multilateral agreement, perhaps alongside or through the International Monetary Fund. A loan can replace some dependency on private finance and reduce the need to cut in the short term. However, when there is a structural problem, as inevitably there will be in such circumstances, cuts cannot be put off entirely. To ensure that the necessary steps are taken to restore fiscal sustainability eventually, international bailouts are about more than just a loan. Conditionality controls the requirements in exchange for the money, which may be released in multiple stages to ensure the meeting of promises. Conditions are usually about fiscal consolidation actions and what structural reforms would fix some of the deeper rooted economic problems. The loss of sovereignty this entails can be a high political price that is not paid lightly.

Within a nation state, there are not normally problems transferring resources from poorer areas to richer ones, or smoothing out slight differences in the economic cycle between them. That is because nations normally have citizens with a common sense of identity that makes it politically possible to have the systems in place to automatically do this. The euro area is a prime example where this isn't the case. It has a common currency but no fiscal transfer union to smooth out differences. That is sometimes described as a silly oversight to correct, but the reason this arrangement ultimately exists is that a single European sense of identity doesn't exist. There is, therefore, no political legitimacy to automatically transfer money from one country to another at whim. Doing so would breach some national constitutions, including Germany's. Without the legitimacy to formalise a transfer union, the single monetary policy setting is unable to correct for cyclical divergences between member states, which led to the euro area's sovereign debt crisis.

During that debt crisis, the transfer problem was well known, but the ability to solve it was constrained severely by the underlying lack of legitimacy. Nonetheless, an attitude of "needs must" developed that saw the creation of a series of bailout vehicles. The first was backed up by the European Union's budget, which relied on non-euro area members providing support too. Bailing out profligate southern European states with excessively generous welfare systems and inefficient workers did not sit well in the UK, but this agreement was reached in the dog days of the Labour government ahead of the 2010 general election. The UK would not sign up to the schemes that followed it with vastly increased sizes to match the much larger problems that had developed. Enhanced cooperation procedures now make it easier for a group of countries to make additional agreements alongside the EU's formal treaties. As it stands, though, better cyclical and structural support systems exist, but nothing comes close to a formal fiscal transfer union. The burden necessarily remains on monetary policy to assist, despite difficulties in directing it at such problems and the question of legal legitimacy within the European Treaties.

Main Messages

- When times are hard, the electorate is prone to demand something be done about it. Direct intervention by capping prices, rationing, wage controls, taxes or subsidies can all seem like natural appeasements.
- Interventions, including price caps and minimum wages, carry costs that can leave output and employment lower than otherwise. There are distributive effects, but there is typically an overall deadweight loss.
- Taxes and subsidies are sometimes calibrated to internalise social costs within the related companies, where it will influence the targeted level of output and prices. However, most taxes exist just to raise money for all the government's wish list of expenditure.
- Automatic fiscal stabilisers arise from the tax and benefit systems. By making most taxation on flows of activity rather than the stock of wealth,

an economic slowdown reduces tax demands. Slower growth also raises unemployment, causing benefits to kick in. Both help smooth spending.

- Discretionary stimulus is sometimes necessary. As people are not perfectly forward-looking, they do not anticipate future tax rises and restrict current spending (i.e. Ricardian equivalence doesn't hold in practice). Nonetheless, there is an opportunity cost from what the private sector would have done, so fiscal stimulus should still seek a real productive return.
- The electorate values personal and economic freedoms, but there is a variable amount that they are willing to give up. Political sustainability of interventions might extend with propaganda that shifts the blame, potentially as justification for more interventions.
- Good politics often involves triangulating to the centre ground between a party's core vote and what the opposition proposes. Scenarios for how political vacuums might develop and influence policy drifts can be informative.
- Ability to finance spending is the ultimate arbiter of sustainability and that tends to be enforced by financial markets (i.e. "bond vigilantes"), albeit far less frequently than it is forecast.
- There is a state-dependent optimal speed of consolidation that is slower than market demands might necessitate, albeit still faster than some statist-biased defenders maintain. International support with conditionality on consolidation and structural reforms can smooth the adjustment.

Further Reading

Bastiat, Frédéric. 1850. *The Law.*

Mankiw, N. Gregory. 2015. *Macroeconomics.*

Rothbard, Murry. 1962. *Man, Economy, and State, with Power and Market.*

Mirrlees, James. 2011. *Reforming the Tax System for the 21st Century: The Mirrlees Review.* Institute for Fiscal Studies.

5
Monetary Policy

The government's deployment of fiscal policy is in some senses the first mover, not least because of automatic stabilisers by definition kicking in automatically. It is also the first mover, though, in that the government has the democratic legitimacy to do what it wants and its delegated agents have to take that as given. Monetary policy has become one of those areas delegated to independent committees in most countries over the past few decades. Under the remit provided, policymakers must merely attempt to mop up any problems that conflict with the target afterwards, primarily by changing the interest rates. As the checks and balances of the political process tend to prevent a prompt discretionary fiscal policy response, monetary policy is typically able to respond to shocks quicker understanding that reaction function is a core part of financial markets. Guidance from policy committees is helpful, but also potentially powerful in its own right. This chapter will explore the relevant aspects of targets and reaction functions before addressing some of the less conventional issues of balance sheet management, which are becoming ever more important.

5.1 Targets

Like fiscal policy, monetary policy affects demand and can be used to smooth out cyclical economic shocks. That doesn't do its effect on financial markets' justice, though. Monetary policy moves interest rates, and this affects markets through direct and indirect channels. An understanding

P. Rush, *Real Market Economics*,
https://doi.org/10.1057/978-1-349-95278-6_5

of the monetary policy transmission mechanism reveals why, but is also necessary for anticipating potential blockages. The transmission mechanism is only a means to an end, though, which need not even be demand itself. Indeed, most developed countries have chosen to delegate monetary policy to control inflationary pressures independently. Other targets are possible and often discussed. This section will explore the transmission mechanism and types of target in turn.

5.1.1 Transmission Mechanism

When monetary policymakers decide to change interest rates, demand in the economy is affected via multiple channels. The attractiveness of savings changes, which determines how much demand defers to the future. Interest payments potentially change, which influences the resources available to spend elsewhere and whether some investments are worthwhile by extension. Domestic asset prices change by the different discounting of future income streams, which leads to wealth effects on current expenditure. And the foreign exchange rate can also be affected. All of these channels might not always be working, and the relevance of each will vary by country, but monitoring of all of them should occur while being mindful that the announcement effect will be small if the policy change is already widely expected.

The savings channel is one of the most important ways interest rates influence demand. When interest rates are high, there is an incentive to save more as those cash balances will attract more income. When rates are low, there is less point in putting off spending rather than doing so now. This effect is intertemporal substitution in that interest rate changes lead to demand being pulled forward or pushed back relative to when it might otherwise have occurred. The underlying time preference of the country's citizens affects what is neutral here. Inflation expectations are also important. If that is expected to be high, interest rates will also need to be relatively elevated to allow real purchasing power to rise by an attractive amount through deferred consumption.

Changes in interest rates also affect cash flow and the level of available disposable income by extension. Higher interest rates mean that borrowers will be paying more to service those debts. It also means that savers will be receiving more income on their savings, but because borrowers are more likely to spend a marginal change in their income than savers are, the borrower's experience is the dominant one overall. Investment decisions are also affected by this as the expected return on investment, adjusted for risk premia, needs to compensate for the cost of borrowing. Higher borrowing costs make it harder for investment projects to clear the hurdle rate of return, which can prevent some projects from being undertaken. Because an expanded capital stock should allow for more production, some economists fear higher interest rates depress supply as well as demand and always advocate loose monetary policy. Investments have to be productive, though, and those projects only viable at meagre interest rates are likely to be those at the greatest risk of failing in the future, so higher rates also prevent some of that pain.

Wealth effects also help transmit monetary policy. The current price of financial assets can be described as the discounted present value of future cash flows. Discounting of future cash flows deepens as interest rates increase, which weighs on the current asset price. Reduced asset values at a time when debt costs are rising represent a wealth squeeze from both sides, which can cause concerns significant enough to cut spending. Moreover, reduced asset values anyway limit the potential for asset sales to fund consumption and investment. In countries where financial asset ownership is high, like the USA, wealth effects can be quite significant. Many other nations, particularly in Europe, have banks intermediating to the extent that the wealth channel is very weak. Housing wealth can often be far larger than financial wealth, but housing is an illiquidity necessity, so the wealth effect from this is relatively small.

With higher interest rates trimming current asset prices but raising the expected value of future coupon payments, international investors are encouraged to chase higher rates in a so-called carry trade. This flow of funds from abroad lifts the foreign exchange rate, which affects the competitiveness of the economy. Imports appear cheaper while exports become more expensive and so less attractive to foreigners. Higher interest rates also, therefore, work through an exchange rate channel. In the same way that countries have different underlying time preferences and propensities to consume from wealth, there are also differences in how important this channel is. High import content and a low price sensitivity to final value added would weigh on the responsiveness of export volumes while small, undiversified economies will be less able to substitute imports for cheaper local alternatives. The currency denomination of external trade and the length of contracts, included hedges, will also influence the responsiveness of prices. In the short term, prices tend to be more flexible than volumes, so higher rates might support demand but should subtract from it eventually. The payoff from this channel theoretically follows a "J-curve", which complicates the transmission mechanism, but it remains an important part of it all the same.

5.1.2 Types of Target

Savings, cash flow, wealth and the foreign exchange rate are all channels interest rates affect demand through. However, none of these things, including demand itself, need to be the basis of the policymaker's target. When politicians control monetary policy, there is nonetheless a temptation to deploy the loose policy to stoke demand ahead of a general election. Removing this temptation to misalign monetary policy towards the political cycle is one of the main reasons for delegating it to an independent committee. Developed democratic countries don't normally have a problem with this, and so independence has increasingly become the norm. Politicians instead chose what the target will be and leave the independent committee to do whatever is appropriate to meet that target. Without political meddling, market participants consider the target to be more credible, and so pricing can focus on what it expects policymakers to do to deliver on it.

By far, the most common form of monetary policy target is consumer price inflation. Because interest rates affect the level of demand much more than supply, policy changes influence the margin of effective spare capacity. That, in turn, affects inflation via the Phillips curve relationship discussed in Chap. 3.2. Controlling demand, therefore, becomes a way of influencing inflation. By setting the inflation target typically near to 2%, businesses and households should not need to spend too much time worrying about the rate of inflation. Such worries can otherwise distort behaviour in unhelpful ways, like having to build inflation risk premia into contracts and wage settlements more likely to be indexed, which itself raises the risk of self-fulfilling wage-price cycles. By maintaining a little bit of inflation in the target, though, nominal rigidities in wages and interest rates themselves are unlikely to bind as frequently, so the economy should run slightly smoother. In other words, high inflation is bad, but a little bit helps grease the economy's wheels.

An extension of the conventional inflation target is to focus on a trend in the price level instead. In this regime, a 2% trend might be set and a period of above-target inflation would need to be followed by a period of below-target inflation to bring the price level back to its trend. Similarly, a time below target would require a period of brisker inflation. The advantage of this regime is that businesses and households always know where they're going to end up. In particular, a period of persistently low price and wage inflation would not leave the burden of debt levels on a permanently more painful path. An unwind would fix it. That does mean that inflation between years could be more volatile owing to payback, but the theoretical issue of volatile inflation raising risk premia and trend inflation may not apply here. More fundamentally problematic is the burden that it places on monetary policy in response to supply shocks. If a negative supply shock devalues the exchange rate, importing inflation, monetary policy will need to be tighter than under a standard inflation target because the inflationary shock on the price level will need to unwind. Either way, a hit to real wages needs to occur, but an inflation target allows for more of that adjustment to come through prices relative to a price-level target, which pushes the pain on to volume adjustments.

Partly because of the effect that interest rates have on demand as well as inflation, some economists argue that both should be a formal part of the target variable. It is the nominal incomes that determine how much people can sustainably afford to increase expenditure by, so there is a logic to making either this or nominal GDP the target. If an increase in inflation squeezes real incomes and demand to the extent that nominal demand is little changed, then policymakers have the inbuilt flexibility to look through the shock. However, trend changes in real potential growth would necessitate a shift in trend inflation to maintain the same pace of nominal GDP growth. This change is only unproblematic under some spurious circumstances, like if potential GDP growth is extremely stable. Or if potential growth is entirely predictable and inflation expectations can be costlessly fine-tuned by the word of a central bank, it would also be fine. Or if growth in the money supply has an exploitable stable relationship with nominal activity, as more of these advocates assume, then nominal targets might work. Unfortunately, none of these things is realistic, and so it has remained mainly an academic debate rather than a real-world policy one.

One way of ensuring that central banks don't become inflation nutters unconcerned about the effect it might have on demand is to include a secondary target on exactly that in the remit. Something along the lines of supporting demand or not causing excessive volatility in it is the kind of compromise that puts some minds at rest. It at least provides cover in the remit to policymakers looking through temporary inflation shocks. Because any inflation targeter is trying to balance demand relative to supply, there is not necessarily a big difference in practice, though. Either way, large positive or negative output gaps require a policy response. Anticipating the size and timing of that change is an essential mixture of art and science that will be explored in Sect. 5.2. Most people don't have the time or interest to focus on such things, though, so policymakers are also prone to providing forward guidance, the specificity of which can vary wildly.

5.1.3 Forward Guidance

The vaguest form of forward guidance is to merely state that the central bank will do what is necessary to meet its target. That leaves the size and timing of any policy change open to interpretation. When applied to an official inflation target, it could be easily misinterpreted by the general public, which risks them being poorly prepared to withstand a policy change, but it should at least reinforce the credibility of the target. Sometimes, the openness of the threatened response can be a good thing. When the ECB famously promised to do "whatever it takes" to preserve the euro area's monetary union, market participants feared to be on the wrong side of that response. They feared it so much that the market pressures dissipated without the central bank needing to launch a shockingly new policy. The forward guidance did the heavy lifting instead.

Policymakers can also help guide expectations on the size and timing of any policy change by discussing the nature of the shocks hitting the economy and what aspects are concerning or not. If it believes an inflation shock is temporary, it can say so and avoid building expectations of tighter policy. When disinflationary spare capacity is seen in unemployment or elsewhere, this can also be highlighted, perhaps alongside expectations for equilibrium levels, including for the policy rate. With the interest rate needing to be about neutral when there is no spare capacity left, assuming inflation expectations are well anchored, such guidance helps indicate the policymaker's perspective on these central judgements. Such guidance says much more about the level of rates in a couple of years than the timing of any adjustment, though.

It is, of course, possible to provide more formal guidance on the timing of any policy change beyond this or the vagueness of "extended period" type statements. The vast array of economic indicators could be simplified down into a form of threshold guidance. For example, in August 2013, the Bank of England stated that it would not hike interest rates until unemployment had fallen below 7%. Conditionality around financial stability or de-anchoring of inflation expectations can provide some simple knockouts on the guidance to shield against material adverse consequences. Other forms of conditionality can be added, which may make the guidance more realistic but at the cost of also making it harder to anticipate when the conditions are met. Such conditional forward guidance is sometimes called "Delphic" after the predictions of the Oracle of Delphi. It is just traditional guidance about the policymaker's expected policy outlook without commitment.

Like the Oracle, a group of sage interpreters is still needed to interpret the predictions, albeit without the need to do so from the hysterical rantings of an intoxicated old lady. Publication of predicted interest rate paths can reduce the role of such sages to forecasting the difference in the economic outlook and the central bank's response to that difference. Nobody can know the reaction function of a policymaker to a given scenario, like the one used in the central bank's forecast, better than the policymaker.

The next level of guidance is to remove some conditionality. This is sometimes known as Odyssean, after the fabled king who bound his hands to the mast of his ship to resist temptation from the sirens. If a central bank can credibly commit to keeping interest rates at a level for a specified period, the market would price in a reduced probability of increases and therefore lower rates. Consumption and investment should be encouraged by this additional stimulus, which would use up disinflationary spare capacity sooner. In doing so, economic conditions would warrant a swifter adjustment in interest rates than would otherwise be the case. A temptation to renege on that commitment in the future would then arise after the benefit has been enjoyed, hence the need to tie the policymaker's hands metaphorically. There is a time inconsistency problem where what is desirable to say now need now be optimal longer-term. And it is especially problematic because it may be different people being bound by the policy than those who initially announced it.

The only credible way of committing to such an approach is to embed it into the target, by referencing trend levels of prices or nominal GDP. A period of weak growth needs to be caught up by a period of stronger growth. That itself implies a need for monetary policy to be looser than it would have been in normal times because achieving a trend pace of growth is temporarily insufficient in those circumstances. Short of embedding commitment within the target itself, forward guidance is ultimately just that: guidance. It is not irrevocable, and it can evolve as things change. Maybe it will be broken, extended, dropped or changed entirely. Understanding the circumstances when this might be the case will help anticipate the next move. Most of the time there won't be such a formal set of signals in the guidance, though, and then an understanding of the reaction function only becomes more necessary. Financial markets rarely price policymakers at their word, and the truth is usually different from either the guidance or the pricing. One must learn the art of reading the runes, assisted by an underlying science that is at best poorly understood by the uninitiated, who may not even realise it exists.

5.2 Core Reaction Function

The ultimate effect of any shock to the economy can be diluted, distorted or even inverted by policymakers, so their reaction function to those shocks needs consideration. Anticipating the shock is not enough to know the effect on the economy or financial markets. Monetary policy is at least a relatively small toolkit compared to the fiscal or macroprudential ones. That simplifies its analysis somewhat because there are fewer dimensions to consider. And compared to commentary on fiscal policy, research on monetary policy is refreshingly short on political bias, albeit not bias overall. The analysis aimed at monetary policy is abundant and subsumed into the core of what good macroeconomists do. Some basic rules of thumb are often used to calibrate expectations for the interest rate outlook and how policy rates might respond in certain scenarios. None can be relied upon, though, with adjustments often needed to make rules fit the prevailing circumstances. Individual policymakers might do this differently or anyway perceive the optimal trade-off differently. This trade-off and the interaction of domestic policy with global events are explored slightly later in this section.

5.2.1 Setting Interest Rates

Monetary policy and interest rates are often used interchangeably among financial market participants. Since the Great Recession of 2008–2009, there has been more to it than that, with quantitative and qualitative easing joining the lexicon and indeed this chapter in Sect. 5.3. Throughout, though, there is at least one policy interest rate that percolates out through wholesale financial markets and potentially on to the interest rates facing real households and businesses. The mechanics of this financial market process are discussed in Part 3. What matters here is that there is an interest rate that policymakers can change to meet their target using the economic transmission mechanism discussed in the previous section. Finding the right level for that interest rate now and in the future is the problem at hand.

The most famous guide for the policy rate is the Taylor rule. It used to provide a reasonable explanation for why policy had done what it did. However, that is the easy bit. Rationalising what has happened can help anticipate the future, but if it is done without carefully decoupling the dynamic parts from the exploitable static relationships, it can be woefully misleading. At the core of the Taylor rule is that inflation targeting central banks have a trade-off between inflation and output. Above-target inflation puts upward pressure on the appropriate interest rate while a shortfall of demand relative to potential provides downward pressure. In the original 1993 version, equal weight was given to inflation and output shocks, but this itself depends on the reaction function of the policymakers and need not be constant through time.

A common mistake is to say that inflation or GDP growth is high and that the policy rate is therefore too low, but this is only true in a relative sense. An increase in GDP growth or inflation implies that the interest rate might need to be a bit higher than it otherwise would have been, but that is not the same as saying a change is needed. Interest rate levels should focus on gaps and levels, not the dynamic pace of the economy. If the potential growth rate is also robust, then demand may not be excessively stimulated. Even with weak potential growth, if the level of output is a long way below potential, interest rates should be at low levels to stimulate demand back to its potential. Failure to do this would leave disinflationary spare capacity that could cause a miss of the inflation target. The value of the dynamic data here are their indications of the gaps and levels that matter, and they do so in a directly observable and less uncertain way than the various bits on the supply side of the Taylor rule.

The deviation of inflation from the target is arguably the most straightforward of the components in this policy rule. Consumer prices are observed and recorded in a not entirely accurate way, but by comparing it to the target for inflation and using the rule as a guide to meet it, the errors broadly balance. The problem is that consumer price inflation is a backward-looking variable. A one-off positive or negative shock to inflation would be relatively unlikely to be incorporated into wage settlements, from where the shock would have affected real incomes and growth. An upside shock would squeeze real incomes and demand, which might weigh on inflation further out, so tightening in response to that would be a mistake.

Augmentations to the inflation measure might be appropriate to understand the policymaker's response better. A one-off shock could be stripped out, but there are always shocks and doing so risks making arbitrary and unreliable value judgements. Various measures of core inflation might be used instead, but where non-core components are persistently adding or subtracting from that core, reliance on a core measure in the rule risks systematically aiming wide of the inflation target. Ultimately, what we're searching for is the level of short-term inflation expectations that are effective in the economy. Expectations can be self-fulling, but they are also unobserved and should ideally be backed out from wage data. Market pricing for inflation-linked instruments can be affected by liquidity, and survey measures are typically asking the wrong people. Nonetheless, if policymakers have a preferred way of looking at inflation expectations, then this should at least be explored. Likewise, potential GDP is unobserved, but the effect of spare capacity can be backed out and used in the other explanatory part of the Taylor rule. Guidance from policymakers on the way they prefer to look at this can be invaluable.

Even for the interest rate itself, there is not a simple constant level of stimulus emanating from any given rate. It is the deviation of effective rates in the economy from their neutral setting that matters here, where that neutral interest rate is the one that would cause the economy to grow at its potential pace. As with potential growth and the level of actual inflation expectations, the neutral interest rate cannot be observed. Because the effect of spare capacity can be observed, changes in the implied margin of spare capacity indicate the effective amount of monetary stimulus. The policy rate is naturally known so adding on this gap provides an estimate of the neutral policy rate. However, there is another missing component here. Consumers and businesses don't typically borrow or lend at anything like the policy rate, and so the spreads to the actual rates quoted in the economy should be added on to both. By incorporating these spreads, the effect that changes in the policy rate have on those interest rate spreads can be factored in and the effective monetary setting anticipated. After all, to know how far interest rates will move, the effect of any change in interest rates on its deviation from a neutral setting needs to be understood.

One side of each of the core variables here is unknown—i.e., the neutral interest rate, potential GDP and inflation expectations, in the respective terms for the effective monetary setting, the margin of spare capacity and deviation from the inflation target. That creates a problem for policymakers in itself. What seems like the right thing to do with the current vintage of data might seem wildly inappropriate with the benefit of hindsight. Rather than risk making large reversals in policy, the optimal approach is often to smooth the response, but it depends on what the costs of being wrong are. The relative costs of inaction are state dependent. Perceptions of the trade-off by policymakers in those different states is itself a crucial part of the overall reaction function.

5.2.2 Trade-offs

Monetary policymakers with an inflation target must trade off deviations from their target against the costs of bringing it back into line. Perceptions of the optimal trade-off are personal to the policymaker, subject to some

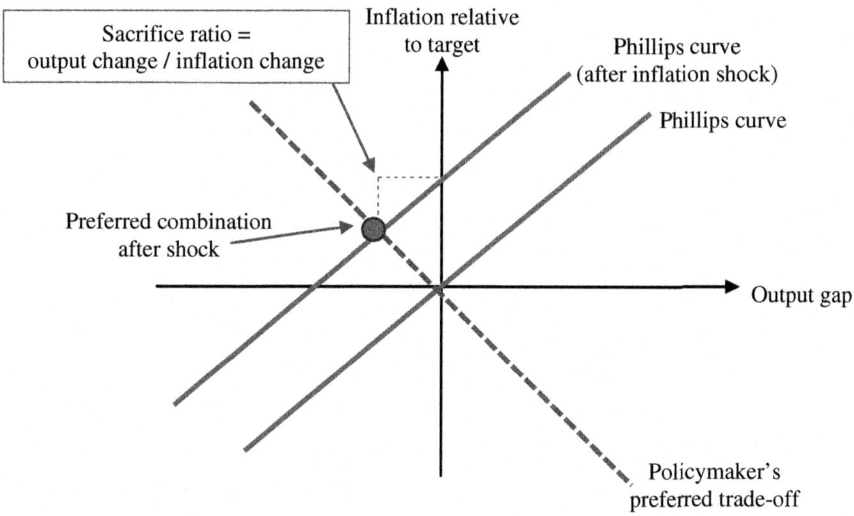

Fig. 5.1 Preferred trade-off

bounds around needing to achieve the target eventually. Different opinions are visible in the different degrees of tolerance for inflation to drift away from the target, both regarding the drift's absolute size and its persistence. When policymakers are called "hawks" or "doves", this trade-off is one of the main underlying traits considered. Fundamentally divergent views on the economy are the other main underlying reason for that moniker to be used. Anything that would cause them to prefer relatively tight (hawkish) or loose (dovish) policy will do, though. Market participants aren't usually shy with slang or simplifying narratives.

Formalising this trade-off between inflation and output is possible. When inflation is expected to be relatively high over policy-relevant horizons, a degree of spare capacity (i.e., a negative output gap) will be needed to counteract that eventually. There is, therefore, an inverse relationship between the policymaker's preferred trade-off between inflation and the output gap (Fig. 5.1). The slope of this line is the trade-off that the policymaker is indifferent between and relates to what is sometimes called the "lambda".

The preferred trade-off is not fixed forever. Changes in the composition of monetary policy committees might shift the collective lambda. Individuals might also change their view of the trade-off if it becomes apparent that the power of monetary policy has changed. A flatter Phillips curve would mean that demand has less effect on inflation so larger changes in interest rates would be needed to drive a bigger change in output just to get the same effect on inflation. The policymaker may then decide that correcting a given

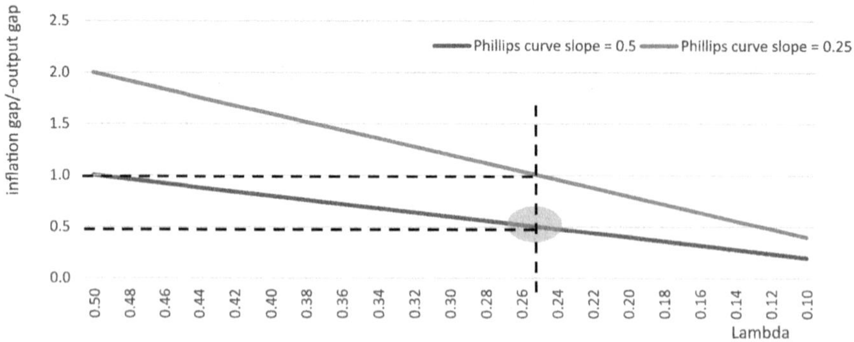

Fig. 5.2 Preferences and the Phillips curve

overshoot in inflation is not worth the output cost and be less likely to respond to it. Indeed, if the Phillips curve slope halves from 0.5 to 0.25, the policymakers would be more tolerant of inflation overshoots at twice the size, provided that inflation expectations remain well anchored (Fig. 5.2).

When developments drive the economy's state to a point away from this preferred line, a policy response might be motivated to draw the economy back into line with a state that it is content to see. There is not some constant level of deviation from this preferred trade-off before a policy response is triggered, though. Treating the trade-off as two dimensional between inflation and the output gap is simplifying away the uncertainty that unavoidably exists. In particular, spare capacity is not directly observed or knowable with any precision, but there are other similarly significant unobserved variables to consider in a Taylor-rule type context, as discussed earlier in this section. Any policy runs the risk of being inappropriate with the benefit of hindsight, whether that policy is to make a change or make none. There will be an economic cost to either mistake and so the relative costs of either need to be discounted into the decision. Moving policy to correct a perceived small deviation from the preferred trade-off does not make sense when the confidence interval comfortably encompasses that line.

There are numerous scenarios when the costs could skew the policymaker's willingness to look through deviations from their preferred trade-off. For example, if the fear is that the economy is entering recession and market expectations have pushed forward rates down relative to the prevailing policy rate, there is an additional asymmetric cost to waiting. Banks' interest margins are squeezed, which can starve the economy of credit while the policymaker holds fire. Alternatively, when the economy appears healthy but not conclusively so, while inflation expectations remain anchored, then policymakers have more time to wait and see what is happening. Indeed, this is one reason why interest rate cuts tend to come much faster than increases. Delaying interest rate hikes is especially encouraged when the policy rate is at or near its effective lower bound. If monetary policy lacks the ability to stimulate away any mistaken tightening, the costs of that mistake will be higher than otherwise. Any disanchoring of inflation expectations is a special case that can cut either way. An aggressive response will be needed to send a signal strong enough to shock those expectations in the desired direction.

When uncertainty is elevated or the perceived costs of an incorrect policy stance are high, it is natural to seek confirmation in measures like wages before changing course. That in effect means looking back to look forward and risks delaying the course change for longer than would otherwise be ideal, but if the costs of error skew in favour of that, then it is still the rational policy to pursue. Postponing course changes can appear inconsistent with the two-dimensional trade-off and is in some senses the more difficult dimension to call. Getting this bit wrong will mean mistaking when changes will occur while the inflation-output Nexus is the bit saying more about the appropriate level of rates. The question that the policymaker will be deliberating on here and that financial market participants need to consider by extension is whether the evidential hurdle rate has been cleared by enough to satisfy the policymaker's intolerance of mistakenly moving policy (Fig. 5.3). Or, in other words, it is the discounted potential cost of hiking too soon less than their intolerance to it.

5.2.3 Global Interactions

So far in this section, the actions of policymakers have been thought of primarily through the domestic lens. Global developments will influence inflation and demand pressures in the economy that the domestic policy responds to, but the interaction of the domestic response to what foreign policymakers do has been sidelined until now. Most economies are open and allow capital to flow freely, so there is a global feedback loop to consider. The most famous model for studying such interactions is the Mundell-Fleming model (also known as the IS-LM-BP model), which is far from perfect, but it is helpful for considering some key concepts. This model is intended to interpret the interactions of equilibrium relationships in the goods (IS: investment and savings), money markets (LM: liquidity preference money supply) and the balance of payments (BP).

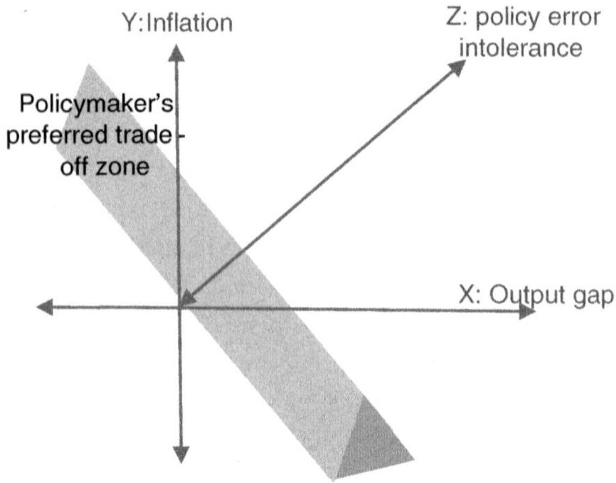

Fig. 5.3 Intolerance as the third dimension

The IS curve is downward sloping because lower interest rates encourage more consumption and investment. Meanwhile, the LM curve is upward sloping because demand for money increases with output and so a higher interest rate would be paid for that given quantity of money. The BP curve is usually upward sloping too, albeit to a reduced degree, because of high levels of demand-increasing imports, which would break the external equilibrium without higher interest rates. Increased levels of capital mobility would flatten this curve as it becomes easier for foreign capital to chase the juicier yield offered domestically. The BP curve is sometimes depicted completely flat, which is to imply perfect capital mobility. An IS-LM intersection above the BP line means a current account surplus while a point below the line is a current account deficit.

A tightening of monetary policy should shift the LM curve to the left as the money supply shrinks, at least in a relative sense. The higher interest rate encourages capital inflows that raise the real exchange rate, which should ultimately squeeze net exports, as depicted by the IS curve moving down to the left. Because domestic assets have become more expensive to foreigners at the higher exchange rate, the BP curve should shift slightly up and to the left. The tightening of policy has therefore reduced activity in the economy, as would have been intended. And the increase in the interest rate will be less than initially implemented because of the global interaction (Fig. 5.4). Similar exercises exist for a monetary loosening, or fiscal scenarios by shifting the IS curve instead.

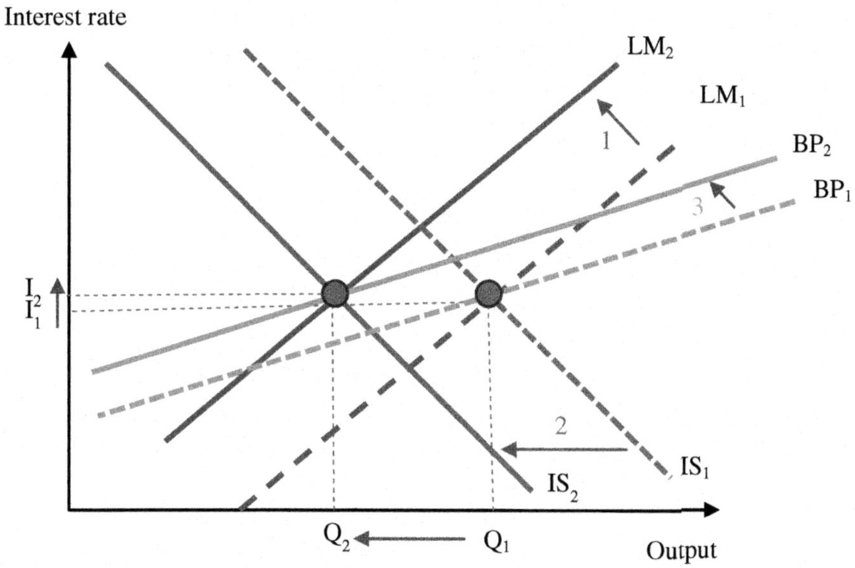

Fig. 5.4 International influences via the IS-LM-BP curves

Trade and financial linkages between countries create spillovers between them that lend cohesion to the global economic cycle. Individual central banks focusing on their domestic situation will often be seeing signals that warrant similar actions to each other. Sometimes, central banks might even coordinate their response in the interests of sending a stronger global message. Under such circumstances, the exchange rate channel is curtailed. Domestic yields don't become more attractive if foreign yields have increased by a similar amount. Because any given national rate is less restrictive than it otherwise would have been, this is a bit like saying that the neutral rate rises during a global tightening cycle. That is in stark contrast to when the hiking cycle is unilateral and the exchange rate response can be potentially so severe as to lower the domestic neutral interest rate.

Foreign exchange rates moves can be highly politically sensitive as they strike at countries' international competitiveness. There can be a temptation to control them, either by explicitly fixing the exchange or by controlling capital flows. By fixing the rate, monetary policy will need to be targeting that instead of things like inflation directly, so any shocks to the economy can't be smoothed out. This limitation can be problematic when exchange rate pressure is coming from developments in the other country. Potentially painful real adjustments still need to be made domestically. But by fixing the exchange rate, the credibility of the other central bank is imported, which can be more beneficial for some countries, especially if foreign trade is mostly denominated in the other country's currency. Fixed exchange rates are a legitimate option for developing countries. What isn't an option is fixing the exchange rate, having free movement of capital and an independent monetary policy. That is the so-called impossible trinity.

For an inflation targeter, monetary policy is independent, and the dynamism of a flexible exchange rate and capital controls tend to be desirable enough for both to be allowed. They must do this subject to the 3-dimensional trade-off discussed in the previous section (i.e., inflation, the output gap and intolerance of error). The interactions of the domestic policy setting with global peers also need to be considered, not least because it can create a state-dependent feedback on to the neutral interest rate. With spreads to quoted rates also potentially dependent on the policy rate setting and uncertainty in each of the three constituent gaps in the Taylor rule, judgement is inevitably needed. Forecasting the central bank reaction function can require some artistic flair, but there is also the aforementioned science beneath it that can be applied in anticipation of potential policy changes and the market movements that will flow from it.

5.3 Balance Sheet Management

Changing the policy interest rate is a tried and tested form of monetary policy, but there is a bit more to it than just moving an interest rate and hoping for the best. For starters, there is often more than one interest rate. They will usually track each other, but the spreads between them can have a real effect on the policy setting, and under certain circumstances, the dominant rate determining the policy setting can even change. Among other things, Chap. 7 will explore how this occurs in the context of the initial transmission of monetary policy transmission to short-term wholesale market interest rates. Sometimes no amount of tinkering with short-term interest rates is enough to deliver the degree of stimulus required. If effective interest rates cannot fall far enough relative to the prevailing neutral rate, the level of demand stimulus will fall short. Then a range of quantitative or qualitative easing measures may be needed.

5.3.1 Quantitative Easing

When the policy rate reaches levels where it cannot be cut much or any further, monetary policy must stop focusing so much on the price of money and instead seek to expand the quantity of money. Quantitative easing involves the central bank buying assets by crediting the facilitating bank's accounts with new reserves at the central bank. These liabilities of the central bank are the highest credit and liquidity quality since the central bank cannot go bankrupt in a conventional sense and reserves will always remain interchangeable among those with accounts at the central bank. Unless politicians choose to restrict the activities of the central bank, its balance sheet can expand indefinitely, so there should be no doubt about the central bank's ability to create inflation. At some point, recklessly aggressive quantitative easing would trigger hyperinflation, which is everywhere a monetary phenomenon. It requires the currency to become so discredited that no one wishes to hold it, thereby causing the value of all real goods, services and assets to rise rapidly. Massive economic damage is caused in such circumstances, which are thankfully quite rare.

The levels of quantitative easing conducted by independent central banks have tended to have had the opposite problem and created insufficient inflation. By buying only the debt of the local sovereign, this is the most allocatively neutral form of quantitative easing. The choice of how to distribute resources is outsourced to the fiscal authority, who has the democratic legitimacy to place taxpayers' money at risk in this way, and the former bond holders. As the government debt is bought at market prices, purchases at negative yields or sales back into the market at higher yields would lead to a loss, which the taxpayer is typically on the hook to cover. However, the risk and its obscurity are sufficiently low not to make it much of an issue, especially relative to the potential benefits of pursuing quantitative easing. By boosting confidence, improving liquidity, encouraging a rebalancing of financial portfolios into riskier assets and raising the money supply, quantitative easing can stimulate the economy.

Confidence is a crucial but cruel mistress for markets. It is ephemeral enough to be invisible, except in its effect at extremes. When confidence crashes, demand disappears, thereby making it even harder to be confident. By being a function of itself, confidence is inherently nonlinear. Small changes in policy might have no effect on confidence while large ones can trigger a sizeable shift of an inordinately greater relative magnitude. If confidence has disappeared and the regular room to stimulate using interest rates is limited, quantitative easing can provide the sort of shock and awe that shifts confidence and the whole outlook. This shock applies to financial market prices both directly and via the support it provides to consumption and investment. The confidence channel is what makes quantitative easing arguably much better suited to serving as a blunt sledgehammer than a precision tool for making fine adjustments to the outlook.

Additional support comes from the effect that purchases have on financial asset prices. The existence of a large buyer in a stressed environment can provide much-needed liquidity and prevent market prices drifting down to deep discounts in search of a buyer. Even among highly liquid government bonds markets, liquidity risk premia will be depressed, thereby raising the current asset prices. Market makers know that they will have an opportunity to close any bond position they buy from a client through a future sale to the central bank, so they don't need to worry about getting stuck with an uncomfortably large position if another buyer doesn't come around when needed. Central banks often intend for it to be real money investors selling their government bonds to it, but banks are a necessary intermediary that might impede the neat transfer of credit to those who might spend it elsewhere. A market-making desk that is clearing its position merely gains room to take the risk again in the same market, perhaps with risk limits even increased slightly relative to what they otherwise would have been because of the backstop and greater profitability.

Even if a real money investor is not in direct receipt of the quantitative easing money, they are the ultimate owners of most bonds so will have benefitted indirectly. And with the price of the assets bought by the central bank being bid up, the relative attractiveness of other asset classes can increase. This effect is the portfolio rebalancing transmission channel. Many academic papers consider it to be one of if not the single most powerful way for QE to support the economy. It relies on the holders of government bonds to be willing and able to switch into other asset classes, though, which isn't true in most cases. Most government bond fund managers cannot change into other assets. The share of the portfolio delegated to that area could be shifted by the CIO or those clients providing the portfolio manager with the cash to invest on their behalf, but this is a slow process with many frictions. Many bonds are also held by pension funds or insurers who have liabilities linked to interest rates too and are required to hold bonds to cover that risk. When running a deficit, as most UK defined benefit pension funds are, for example, the reduction in yield can raise liabilities by more than the assets and prompt a further allocation towards government bonds to reduce the deficit. The natural habitat of investors can at least curtail the effect of this channel, where the degree will vary by market and bond maturity.

The direct effect of additional central bank money in the system is also arguably a support to growth via increased credit creation. American monetarists tend to see the newly created central bank money as high powered, which will then be levered up into the broader money supply. However, that supposes that banks are short of liquid asset reserves, which ceases to be the case once the central bank chooses to increase their supply far beyond what is naturally needed. There is still an increase in the money supply because where a bond holder is selling the asset to the central bank via a commercial bank, the commercial bank is credited with a central bank reserve and it, in turn, credits the original bond holder's account with newly created commercial bank money. This process might seem surprisingly abstract at this stage, but the different sorts of money and its creation shall be discussed further in Chap. 8. For now, the main point here is simply that this channel is only directly effective in an environment that is unlikely to exist. Otherwise, the effect is just an extension of the portfolio rebalancing one. Some investors have some extra commercial bank money, and they'll probably choose to buy other things with it. But because of who they are, what they're buying is likely to be more bonds and almost certainly more assets, so that money merely raises asset prices rather than demand distinctly and directly.

Some economists take scepticism about the limitations of monetary policy to a greater extreme and argue that monetary policy can be completely ineffective. Such stimulus is like pushing on a string when the economy enters a so-called liquidity trap. Theoretically, a liquidity trap arises from the Keynesian adherence to the "liquidity preference theory", wherein the rate of interest is functionally related to how much cash the public wants to hold. In this view, cash balances are thought to vary with changes in either the transaction, precautionary or speculative motives. So, if people become gloomier, they are likely to hoard more cash as a precaution against losing income by selling speculative holdings. The realisation that negative rates are limited by the inability to charge interest to holders of banknotes can compound speculative selling. At this lower bound, Keynesians believe that demand for money (liquidity preference) becomes so high that it is impossible for monetary policy to stimulate investment enough to get the economy out of recession. In John Hick's IS-LM framework, this is shown by the LM curve, which monetary policy determines, becoming horizontal near the lower interest rate bound (Fig. 5.5).

The liquidity trap was initially about the short-term nominal interest rate, so most of the world would already be branded as in a liquidity trap by those standards. However, the problem arises partly from the shortcomings of the IS-LM model. It is a comparative statics framework that ignores dynamics in addition to inflation and expectations, including of term interest rates. In reality, some stimulus can still be provided by changing expectations of future short rates, which forces longer rates down. The most popular method to escape a liquidity trap, pushed by the likes of Paul Krugman, is the gratuitous use of fiscal stimulus. That should shift the IS curve right and

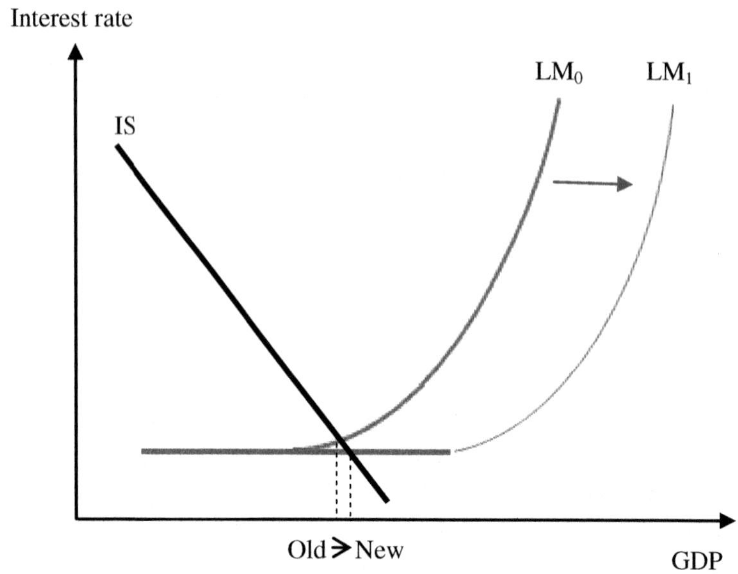

Fig. 5.5 Liquidity trap on the IS-LM curves

insofar as the intersection with the LM curve remains on the flat part, GDP can be expanded without a rise in interest rates. Again, though, it is ignoring the expectations channel. If the structural fiscal deficit becomes large enough to be obviously unsustainable, expectations of default risk will still raise interest rates.

An aggressive expansion of the monetary base via quantitative easing could still boost inflation expectations and drive real yields even lower, but if those expectations were consistent with the target to begin with, shocking them would be in breach of the central bank's mandate. Inflation can be generated much easier than real growth. After all, monetary policy does not determine the labour supply or improve the entrepreneurial decisions driving productivity growth, but instead is mostly just about the intertemporal substitution of demand. Unfortunately, that inflation need not be in the consumer prices officially targeted. If the central bank's bid is for government bonds, that is naturally where a relative shift in the supply-demand balance will drive most inflation to occur. Attempts to channel that demand elsewhere can add a qualitative aspect to the easing, which can extend monetary policy's effectiveness at stimulating demand into some liquidity trap-like conditions.

5.3.2 Qualitative Easing

Quantitative and qualitative easing often go together. The quantitative aspect is the expansion of the money supply, and the qualitative aspect is the increased risk profile of the assets bought. Buying the bonds of the central bank's sovereign is merely a transfer of resources within the public sector. Nonetheless, it could be structured in such a way as to make it more qualitative. Doing so would require coordination between monetary and fiscal policymakers. The central bank could agree to finance the government's fiscal stimulus plan, potentially bypassing the need to issue new bonds in financial markets. Whether or not the bonds related to this stimulus plan cycle through the private sector of not, though, such coordination could still cause an adverse market reaction. If the level of stimulus appears to be a function of the fiscal demand rather than the monetary need, inflation expectations will rise, thereby increasing the cost of all other government borrowings.

The reason such concerns arise amid lost independence is that there are always demands on politicians and the temptation of an active printing press blunts the budget constraint. There is no trade-off between low taxes, support for the poor, infrastructure investment, public services and the pay of its workers if a bit more money can paper over all the problems. In the process, though, the value of the currency can degrade to nothing in a destructive hyperinflationary episode. Those events are everywhere a monetary phenomenon, with political interference motivating the excesses. Provided that the central bank remains in control of the stimulus plan's magnitude, it may not be a problem, but it also relies on it not being perceived as a problem by investors who would then take flight. That is why this sort of proposal typically intends for the central bank to hold a government bond in return for the printed money provided. Not to do so would be pure monetization and seem scarier, although it is not much different in practice. Without a bond to hold, the central bank would be bankrupt, except it has the unique ability to print liabilities that must be accepted, so that isn't a binding problem. And because the state owns the central bank, the government is effectively just offering it an equity claim instead of debt. If monetary policy becomes a tool of the state, there isn't much difference between that equity or debt liability. The government can choose to pay back either or not bother.

One way of maintaining political independence is to provide funds to the real economy without going through the government. This approach is the so-called helicopter drop of new money, which is easier said than done. Knowing what an even distribution of resources is, let alone how to direct funds consistent with it, is an unavoidably difficult question. Inevitably, any "helicopter drop" would create relative winners and losers among an electorate that never elected the monetary policymakers behind the decision. Acting with a democratic deficit is dangerous. Those who lose out are always going to be more vocal than those who benefit, and that could strengthen demands for political interference in the process, which would carry all the usual risks associated with lost independence.

Even if the policy could be delivered in a neutral or democratically acceptable way, the central bank is far from being the best agent to pick winners. Misallocation of resources could easily occur. It is much safer to leave the private sector to make such allocative decisions, thereby leaving the central bank to focus on the effective margin of monetary stimulus. A relatively neutral way of qualitatively increasing the risk profile of the central bank's assets is to buy the liabilities of the private sector, instead of the state's privately held liabilities. For example, corporate bonds or securitized loans can be purchased. Such markets are relatively small, illiquid and are not representative of the wider market on all metrics, though. Some sectors and companies within them will have skewed their issuance plans towards these securities, and they will disproportionately benefit from central bank purchases of them. When supply in the secondary market is short, price moves can be large and the free float of the remaining assets might end up uncomfortably small for others to continue transacting. Central banks can simultaneously support a market with much higher prices and kill it from functioning. When times are bad, and the need for stimulus desperate, any encouragement to issue and invest more might be welcomed, though, irrespective of the damage to the market.

The combined effect of qualitative easing should be to ease financial conditions in the economy. These tend to be measured by a mixture of underlying monetary and credit conditions metrics. On the monetary side, there are short- and long-term government bond yields, as well as the trade-weighted foreign exchange rate. Meanwhile, the credit conditions side includes the spreads relative to those risk-free rates and also equity prices, or some derivative thereof. Financial conditions should be closely related to underlying changes in monetary policy, but that is not always true. Indeed, during the credit boom that preceded the Great Recession, US financial conditions loosened enough to offset the steady increases in the policy interest rate. The sudden tightening of financial conditions in the credit crunch then triggered a recession, despite relative stability in monetary policy. And then in the aftermath when policy rates were cut, pass-through was constrained to the extent that financial conditions loosened by far less than would have been expected based on the change in the short change alone.

Factoring in broader measures of financial conditions might align monetary policy better with the needs of the real economy, and many policymakers now place more emphasis on it, especially in the USA. However, the disinflationary shock from Asian goods exports meant that monetary policy was not excessively loose relative to inflation targets during the credit boom. Monetary policy is typically required to focus on controlling the risks most relevant to its target over the next few years, so there is a residual danger of longer-term imbalances building. The correction of such imbalances can cause a material miss of the monetary policymakers' target, but at a point potentially so far away that it is not necessarily worth trying to correct it using monetary policy instruments. Indeed, if successful, the imbalances won't accumulate and the risks won't crystallise, so monetary policymakers would merely appear to have done the wrong thing with the benefit of hindsight, where the counterfactual can't be seen. Another policy toolkit is needed beyond the blunt instruments of monetary policy. This relatively new toolkit is wielding by the increasingly powerful set of macroprudential policymakers.

Main Messages

- Monetary policy redistributes consumption and investment across time, partly as the attractiveness of savings and the cost of debt are affected by the policy rate. Wealth effects and the foreign exchange rate are also part of the transmission mechanism.
- Central banks are increasingly institutions that set policy independently of government, with an inflation target near 2% most popular of all. By manipulating demand with interest rates, the margin of spare capacity is affected, and inflation is by extension via the Phillips curve.
- A price-level target would provide the public with a better guide as to where prices will end up over long periods, but it would force the real wage adjustment following adverse supply shocks to fall much more firmly upon activity, which may not be desirable.
- Forward guidance can be powerful when it is credible, even if the specificities are missing. Conditional guidance can simplify the range of indicators into those that matter most to the policy decision.

- Attempts to bind future policy votes are often called Odyssean guidance, in contrast to the regular Delphic kind. It suffers from time inconsistency, where what is rational to say for stimulus now can be rational to renege on sooner than would otherwise have been the case.
- Any interest rate rule needs to be tweaked for the prevailing circumstances, which reduces its usefulness. The Taylor rule is the most popular lens to view monetary policy through, which has the trade-off between inflation and the output gap at its core.
- The effect of spare capacity is implied in wage growth, and changes in that margin of slack indicate where interest rates are relative to their neutral setting.
- Policymakers with a preference for relatively tight or loose monetary policy are referred to as hawks and doves, respectively.
- There is an inverse relationship between the policymaker's preferred trade-off between inflation and the output gap. The slope of this line is sometimes called the "lambda".
- Uncertainty is unavoidable, as is the risk that policy appears inappropriate with the benefit of hindsight. When the perceived costs of error are high, the evidential hurdle to changing course is greater. The discounted potential cost of a mistake needs to be less than the policymaker's intolerance to it. That is the third dimension to the policymaker's true trade-off.
- Global interactions also affect the monetary response. Unilateral policy changes cause foreign exchange rate moves that can push the neutral interest rate in the opposite direction, thereby creating a greater change in conditions than would be the case during a global policy cycle.
- There is an impossible trinity, whereby a country cannot have a fixed exchange rate, have free movement of capital and set an independent monetary policy. The choice of what to have will determine how the economy bears real adjustment costs.
- When interest rates can't be cut further, monetary policy must shift focus from the price to the quantity of money and buy assets. A central bank's balance sheet can technically be expanded indefinitely, which means it can always create inflation up to levels of a highly damaging hyperinflation. Creating inflation is much easier than stimulating real demand.
- Quantitative easing can work by boosting confidence, improving liquidity, encouraging a rebalancing of financial portfolios into riskier assets and raising the money supply. It is arguably better suited for shock and awe style confidence shocks than fine-tuning.

- The incentive to rebalance portfolios after central bank purchases is often considered to be the most powerful channel. In practice, limitations on the natural habit of investors mean that the inflation from QE tends to be concentrated in the market purchases take place.
- Sceptics about the ability for monetary policy to stimulate real demand will refer to it pushing on a string once the economy falls into a liquidity trap. Fiscal policy is the usual prescription for escape, but the scenario and solution partly arise from the flaws in the framework being used.
- Qualitative easing can extend the effectiveness of monetary policy. It involves increasing the risk profile of the assets bought. An absence of democratic legitimacy makes it dangerous to take distributive decisions, but coordination with the government is no panacea.

Further Reading

Den Haan, Wouter. 2013. *Forward Guidance*. Vox EU.
Taylor, John B. 1993. *Discretion versus Policy Rules in Practice*.

6

Macroprudential Policy

It is the role of macroprudential policy to smooth out the broad sweeps of the credit cycle. In doing so, horizons far beyond monetary policymakers are considered, although both will affect current behaviours. For this reason, there is sometimes a big overlap between monetary and macroprudential policy committees to prevent them accidentally pushing policies against each other, but that is not necessarily true, and governments continue to hold rather than delegate the policy levers in many countries. Some knowledge of bank balance sheets is required to understand the effects of macroprudential policy. How regulations on capital and liquidity influence these is the starting point of this chapter. The role of more targeted interventions into lending standards will follow it. Finally, for when credit cycles inevitably do turn down, the additional tools available to moderate the shock will be considered.

6.1 Capital and Liquidity Buffers

Like all companies, banks have a balance sheet, which covers all of their assets and liabilities. Assets are things that are owed to the enterprise, while liabilities are what the company owes to others. The asset side of a simplified bank has some loans that are relatively safe and others that are risky, where a portion of those (typically the safest) assets are ones that can be sold quickly without affecting their price—i.e. so-called liquid assets. On the liability side, there are some types of funding that might disappear at short notice

P. Rush, *Real Market Economics*,
https://doi.org/10.1057/978-1-349-95278-6_6

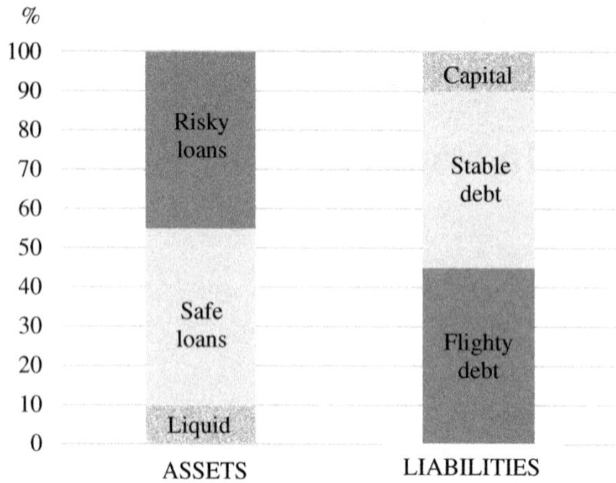

Fig. 6.1 Stylised bank balance sheet

and others that are stable. At the most stable end lies the banks' capital, which it raises through retained earnings and the issuance of equity. Both the asset and liability sides of the balance sheet are necessarily equal and so both need to be considered when anticipating the potential effect of shocks (Fig. 6.1).

6.1.1 Moving Buffers

Creditors to banks are not obligated to stay so indefinitely. Each lender carries a propensity to withdraw that funding. If too much financing disappears, akin to a bank run, the bank faces a credit crunch (Fig. 6.2). Paying back creditors who want their funds back requires selling liquid assets like government bonds and central bank reserves. If the bank holds insufficient liquid assets, it may need to sell other less liquid ones at discounted prices, with adverse consequences. To limit the probability of this, regulators require banks to hold a minimum level of liquid assets. Since the global credit crunch in 2008, many banks have been holding far above this buffer, partly because of the central bank reserves created during QE.

By holding excessively high levels of liquid assets, banks find their balance sheets become bogged down with this, which leaves fewer resources available to lend to the private sector. Lower liquidity requirements might encourage more lending to the real economy, but it might have no effect if they're not initially binding. Or if the obligation did bind behaviour, a cut could cause

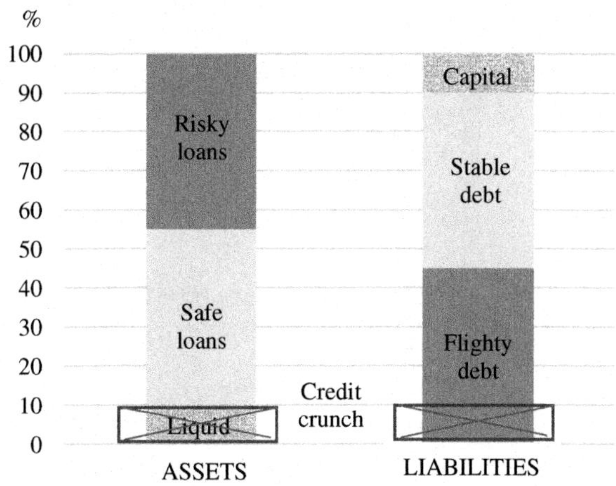

Fig. 6.2 How liquidity buffers are used

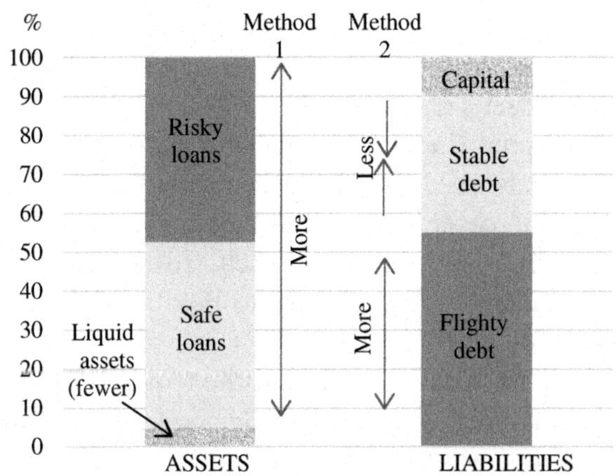

Fig. 6.3 Two ways to meet a lower liquidity coverage ratio

funding strategies to shift towards less stable forms if it is profitable to do so (Fig. 6.3). Whether changes occur on the asset or liability side will depend on the circumstances at the time, including on monetary policy. Central bank reserves have to be held by someone so such systems can determine whether the liquidity requirement is anywhere near binding or not.

Whenever a bank makes a loan, it runs the risk that the borrower will not meet the agreed repayment schedule, forcing the bank to take a loss. Under some circumstances and accounting standards, a change in the expected level of losses is enough to require a bank to incorporate the loss into its

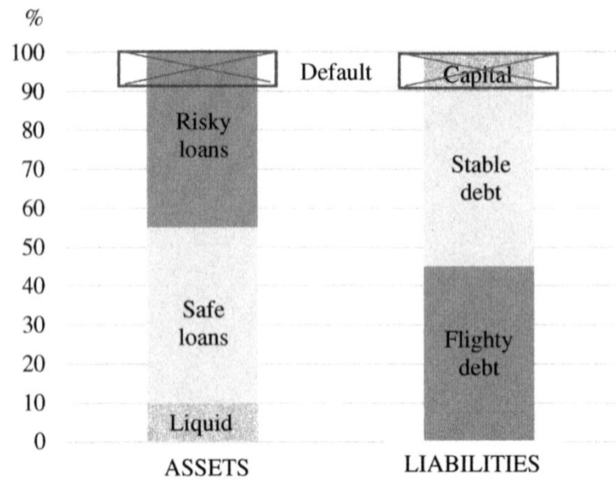

Fig. 6.4 How capital buffers are used

accounts. And as the trading book must be marked to market prices, market revaluations hit the asset values recorded by banks. Profits elsewhere in the business might offset small losses, but where there are losses overall, the bank must use its capital (i.e. equity and retained earnings). Funding from other sources ultimately needs to be repaid to the lender. However, if there is insufficient capital to cover losses, other creditors may be bailed into avoid an insolvent bank disorderly dissolving itself. To reduce the probability of bank insolvency, regulators require banks to hold a minimum level of their own capital (Fig. 6.4).

The experience of the credit crunch and the required bank bailouts motivated policymakers around the world to demand higher minimum capital requirements. The hope was that banks would meet raised targets by issuing new equity, but that is only one of the two ways to achieve a higher capital ratio. Rather than raise capital, a reduction in the balance sheet could shrink the capital requirement. As this was just a risk-weighted issue at the time, the incentive was not to make new risky loans and allow existing ones to roll off. With the equity market value of banks far short of their book value, selling new equity in such an environment would have amounted to indirectly selling the underlying assets at a substantial discount, which most didn't want to do. Some banks were forced to raise or receive new capital injections from the government, most notably in the USA, to bring a swift recapitalisation. For the most part, though, banks had the choice, and they chose a path of de-risking and deleveraging (i.e. Method 1 in Fig. 6.5), which harmed economic growth.

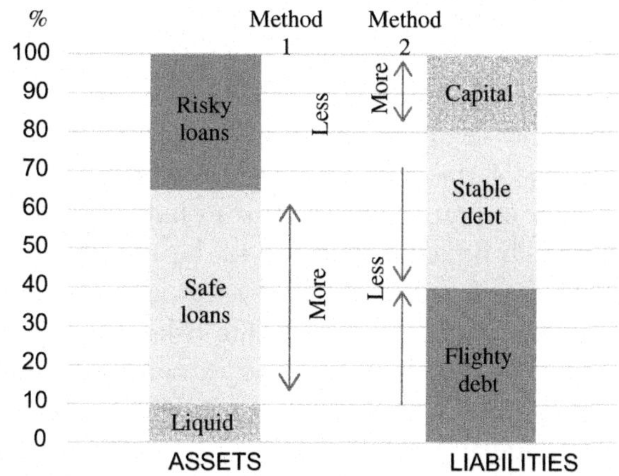

Fig. 6.5 Two ways to meet a higher capital target

6.1.2 The Capital Stack

Regulatory capital requirements are not the same for all banks and would not even be constant for the same bank if it chose to base operations out of different countries. There is a common global framework for capital requirements (i.e. Basel III), but these guidelines are translated into more prescriptive regulations in each jurisdiction. As such, the interpretation of USA, European and other regulators might differ slightly. It can even vary between members of the EU as the European directive on this (CRD IV) is translated separately into the law of each member state. Such differences can create advantages for some banks and this encourages lobbying for loopholes that make meeting capital requirements less onerous for some, with higher profits by extension. Nonetheless, the existence of global standards constrains the room for regulatory divergence, thereby reducing the potential regulatory arbitrage in relocating to areas with a more favourable regime.

A core feature of every Basel Accord has been the variable nature of capital requirements between institutions. In the beginning, this placed broad asset types into five buckets, with different risk profiles and capital requirements for each one. Subsequent iterations introduced far more detail with the aim of better aligning the risk profile of bank holdings with the capital they must hold against them. After all, banks hold different assets, and this means that their exposure to various risks will also differ. When the expected losses in a given scenario are larger, it is natural for that bank to hold more capital to absorb those losses. This requirement is the essence of what is now known as the Pillar 1 capital requirement, which should be held at all times.

As banks provide a valuable service to the public, a failure to have sufficient capital to absorb losses could lead to a bailout using taxpayer money. Socialising losses while the profits remain privatised leaves a social cost that banks might reasonably be made to internalise. That internalisation allows an optimal reduction of this risk. The regulatory framework does this by requiring systemically important institutions to hold more capital. This systemic risk buffer should be set in reference to the additional costs that these institutions would create for the financial system and economy if they were to fail, rather than in relation to the specific risks that the organisation is running. Inevitably, this can lead to some extraordinary diseconomies to scale as banks seek to avoid the costs of being designated systemic.

Together with the Pillar 1 requirement, systemic banks should strive to hold this capital at all times. As shocks hit and the cycle turns, losses will inevitably occur, and so there should also be enough additional capital to withstand these losses without dipping into this regulatory minimum. That way there should be a big enough buffer to prevent investors becoming so concerned about bank solvency that they precipitate the problem by withholding funding to the bank. Within this useable buffer, there are a few forms of capital requirement. Invariable to the institution or the economic cycle is the capital conservation buffer (CCoB), which is 2.5% of risk-weighted assets. As a system-wide adjustment for the economic cycle, macroprudential policymakers are also able to set a countercyclical capital buffer (CCyB). This buffer forces banks to hold more capital when the credit cycle looks to be stretching towards bigger imbalances and more significant losses from their correction. Beyond that are institution-specific buffers that regulators might opt to impose.

Between the CCoB, CCyB and any regulator-imposed top-ups, each bank should have enough capital to withstand the losses incurred during a plausibly stressed scenario, without drawing upon the regulatory minimums discussed previously. One rough but recommended guide for macroprudential policymakers is the credit to GDP ratio, although the sustainable level of this depends on too many things to make it useful. A better approach to calibrating these three useable buffers is that of the Bank of England (BoE), which calibrates the buffers in response to what its annual stress tests yield. Doing it this way allows for much more granular information on the actual exposures and potentially allows for feedback channels between institutions to be incorporated too. Credible stress tests are the best reflection of potential losses in a plausible scenario. The BoE seeks to set the CCyB to a level that gives the banking system enough capital to withstand the systemic losses, after accounting for the CCoB. The difficulty is defining a degree of stress that varies appropriately with the economy's position in the credit cycle and nothing else.

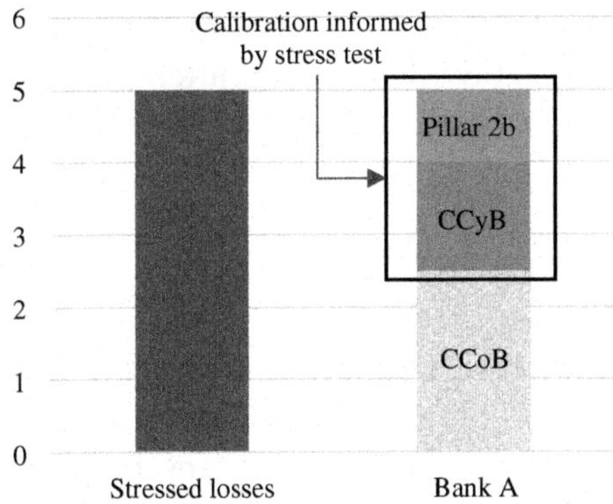

Fig. 6.6 Calibration of the useable capital buffers

Where individual institutions have higher exposure to the plausible stressed scenario, there could be a case for requiring them to hold additional capital. Such capital is designed for use if or when the cycle turns down but ensures that individual banks are not incentivised to run far more risk than the rest of the system. Doing so would lead regulators to require them to hold more capital, which would raise their idiosyncratic costs, potentially to the point where such reckless behaviour becomes unprofitable. This capital is part "b" of the second pillar in Basel III, which sets an additional buffer during the supervisory review process (the third pillar sets disclosure requirements to allow the market to impose discipline). Residual risks that are not directly related to the economic cycle form part "a" of pillar 2. And unlike the cyclical part, Pillar 2a is a minimum requirement that banks are expected to maintain at all times. Implementation of International Financial Reporting Standard 9 (IFRS9) should remove some supervisory concerns about risk weightings, which had previously meant raising Pillar 2 capital requirements. However, some other risks, like legal ones, will likely still be incorporated by various supervisors into this bit of the capital stack (Fig. 6.6).

Setting of capital requirements used to be just in reference to risk-weighted assets, but this might not always be effective. Indeed, the low risk-weighting of mortgages exaggerated the credit boom during the 2000s by making it profitable to leverage up into them, at least until the bubble burst. Regulators fear a concentration of risk developing in erstwhile safe assets that bring about another crisis. As such, a non-risk-weighted approach to calculating and setting capital requirements is useful and known as the leverage ratio. This simple method can also sometimes be applied to countercyclical requirements, to ensure that there is not a relative loosening of this requirement compared to the risk-weighted ones when the credit cycle is extending. The leverage ratio is there as an intentionally simplistic backstop to limit exuberance of the finance sector.

6.2 Lending Standards

Simple rules, like the leverage ratio, are useful backstops to have against underappreciated risks building up across bank balance sheets. However, sometimes the risks are much clearer. Countercyclical capital buffers (CCyB) and institution-specific top-ups under Pillar 2 are ways to control these risks, but they are relatively blunt tools. Neither buffer will target a particular problem, but merely require banks to hold additional capital overall. To the extent that risks are accumulating in an exceptionally profitable area, raising the overall volume and potentially the cost of capital might not have the desired effect. Indeed, it may even encourage further concentration of risk as banks seek higher returns on equity. There is, therefore, a need for an additional set of prudential tools beside the overall capital and liquidity requirements. Some of these are to prevent borrowers overextending themselves, which could also reflect back on the bank in the crisis, while others directly target the resilience of banks.

6.2.1 Borrower Affordability

Banks don't want to lend money to people that won't pay them back. Inevitably, not all borrowers will be able to repay loans as promised, but the aim is nonetheless to avoid knowingly making such loans in the first place. Doing so regardless would be bad for the borrower as well as the lender. As such, before approving a loan, banks assess borrowers against various criteria to ensure that they are likely to be able to repay their loans. However, there are arguably times when banks become overly relaxed about the risks of some investments they are making, which justifies regulatory restrictions in defence of the borrower and bank by extension. The problem could come from plans to sell loans onto others, thereby making the bank much less concerned about eventual losses on the loans. Requirements for the lender to retain a portion of the risk when the loans are sold on internalises some of the default cost and restrains this urge to issue and sell on bad loans.

Insufficient lending standards might also occur when a bank is prioritising market share as this objective dulls their risk management focus. Anticipated high losses on loans may nonetheless be tolerable because of expected economies to scale. While lax lending standards could then be optimal for the bank, they would not be for the borrowers allowed to overextend themselves. Of course, by voluntarily taking the loan, the borrower cannot plead coercion and pass off all blame, but society may wish to protect such people from themselves by preventing banks from ever making such loans. Regulators can do this by setting minimum standards on some of the key variables underlying bank loan approval decisions.

The core question when assessing a loan application is whether the borrower can afford to at least service the debt. This answer is a function of the loan size, its interest rate, the borrower's income and any other commitments they might have. The borrower's financial situation is not something the bank controls beyond the loan it is issuing. That just leaves the pertinent variable of what loan size is affordable given the borrower's disposable income under different interest rate scenarios. Regulators can require plausibly aggressive increases in interest rates to be factored into the assessment to prevent banks from passing loans that are only affordable if monetary policy is excessively stimulative. In addition to or perhaps instead of these affordability assessment scenarios, a cap on the loan to income ratio might be set, which is a simpler version of the same thing. For loans intended to invest in assets, like buy-to-let property, the regulator might impose an equivalent interest coverage ratio to ensure borrowers are not required to inject large amounts of capital on a regular basis just to service the investment.

6.2.2 Bank Resilience

When bad loans are few, it is mainly just bad for the borrower, but when losses are more widespread, it can become more of a problem for the lender. Defaults are likely to be correlated, so the breadth of risky lending must be considered in addition to the depth of credit condition loosening. If assumptions about the average default rate prove wrong, losses could mount and ultimately threaten the bank's solvency. Regulators, therefore, have to worry about the overall exposure of the bank to people who may not have overstretched themselves individually but are part of a pool of individuals with worryingly limited resilience to potential shocks. Limits on the proportion of a bank's loans going to borrowers with riskier characteristics are the natural response in this scenario. For example, the supervisor might say that only 15% of new loans can be to borrowers with a more than a ratio of 4.5 between the loan value and their income. This ratio should constrain the spike in the default rate under certain scenarios and aid resilience.

The default rate alone does not say how much money banks are losing from bad loans. For that, the loss given default is needed, which is related to the recovery rate. Most lending is secured on an asset that the bank can take possession of and sell, typically at some discount to the market price to facilitate a quick sale. With a view to provide themselves with a buffer to make quick sales without losing money, banks typically ask for borrowers to deposit some of their money into asset purchases. That way the borrower takes the first loss in an adverse scenario. Smaller deposits mean risky loans and higher interest rates. Loan products are usually split into buckets using their loan to asset value ratio (LTV). When the regulator is worried about the exposure banks are building up to high LTV lending, it could choose to cap the LTV banks are permitted to lend at or cap the proportion of such loans by the bank. This cap is equivalent to the breadth versus depth analogy used earlier with the high loan to income (LTI) ratio loans.

Discounted quick sales are effective when they are relatively rare, but they become problematic as default rates and repossessions rise. Deeper discounts need to be offered for them to find demand and clear the inventory. That is particularly the case since demand itself is likely to be weaker in an environment where this sort of forced supply is elevated. Provided the asset sells for the value of the loan, the bank is relatively indifferent to how much the asset sells for because that excess would merely flow back to the defaulted borrower. As buyers see deeper discounts on offer with these properties, other sellers could find themselves having also to lower their price to make the sale. In this way, asset prices could be reduced more generally, including those underlying other loans. If those other loans default, it will become increasingly difficult for the bank to recover the value it had lent. And where the borrower's deposit is entirely used up, placing them in negative equity, the incentive to keep up payments might also fall, further raising the default rate and the problem for the banks. Fire sales can feed on themselves like a fire. Banks, borrowers and the regulators would like to avoid these adverse dynamics wherever possible.

6.3 Liquidity Facilities

One of the reasons assets may sell at a discount to the market is because the holder can't afford to hold out for a better price. If cash is needed, but that money is tied up in other assets, there is a liquidity problem to resolve by liquidating assets. Where enough assets can't be sold, or at least not at a reasonable price, the liquidity problem can become an additional solvency one. Forcing erstwhile viable businesses into bankruptcy for temporary cash-flow limitations is not desirable for society and certainly not for the afflicted companies. For this reason, most policymakers favour providing liquidity support, while support during solvency problems is a judgement reserved for politicians who must place taxpayer funds at risk. This doctrine is a long held one perhaps most famously espoused by Walter Bagehot as "Lend without limit, to solvent firms, against good collateral, at high rates".

When the central bank provides liquidity support in this way, it is lending either government bonds, bills, or central bank reserves, which are all highly liquid assets for banks. The banks need to place collateral for use as security for the liquid assets. What types of collateral are acceptable will depend on the liquidity operation. Because of the higher risk profile of the assets used as collateral, the central bank will typically require the placement of more assets than the value of the loan given. The difference is the so-called "haircut" that ensures the central bank does not inadvertently end up facing a loss on the loan that it can't recoup by selling the collateral. Because of the additional assets encumbered by using the liquidity facility, there is a balance sheet cost to the banks of using them. There is also likely to be a direct charge for drawing upon liquidity facilities to discourage frivolous use. The central bank should serve as a lender of last resort during liquidity problems rather than replace functioning markets, although that is sometimes the unfortunate side effect, especially of the system-wide operations.

6.3.1 Institutional Support

Liquidity facilities tend to provide liquid assets in exchange for collateral from an exceptionally extensive eligible universe of assets. This breadth is to ensure that banks don't find themselves unable to participate owing to a shortage of available assets. Some central banks even accept raw loan books. The usual arrangement is for banks to preposition collateral with the central bank so that it can be rapidly called upon if the need arises. The costs of an institution participating will then depend upon what assets they have used and how extensively they are relying on the facility. Some central banks, like in the USA and UK, have set up so-called "discount windows" where banks can go to get liquidity on demand, without having to wait for other regularly scheduled operations, which may not anyway allow the same range of collateral. In the UK's case, the Bank of England defined its discount window's charging schedule for banks and building societies as illustrated in Fig. 6.7, which is naturally open to change whenever it wants.

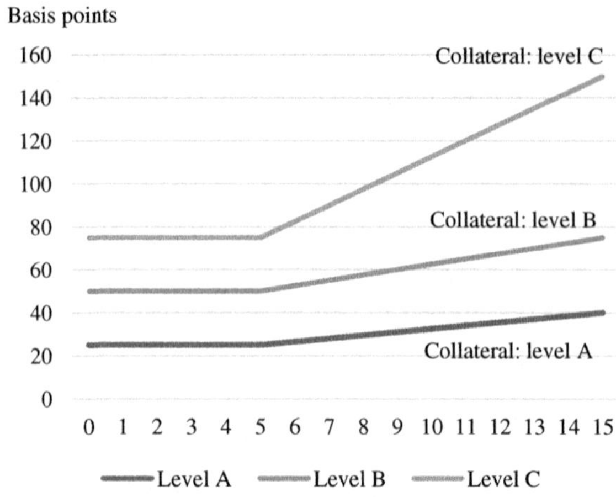

Fig. 6.7 Average discount window facility borrowing cost

For the Bank of England or the US Federal Reserve, there is the simplicity of a single sovereign underwriting it for any potential losses. If a bank was unable to repay the liquid assets lent to it and the collateral was insufficient to cover the gap, the taxpayer would pay (either directly or through reduced profit transfers) without any potential conflict with the central bank's legal standing. As is often the case, things are more complicated in the euro area. Supporting a bank in one country creates a risk that losses will be pooled among other nations. The European Central Bank (ECB) tries to avoid this by making support to specific troubled institutions through emergency liquidity assistance (ELA). National central bank members of the ECB provide ELA support and are responsible for any costs and risks associated with it. As large loans (>EUR2bn) may become inconsistent with the ECB's function, the Governing Council reserves the right to set maximum thresholds for ELA usage by an institution or even several groups of them if there is a more systemic problem.

6.3.2 Systemic Operations

When problems are systemic, central banks often move into a firefighting mode where longer term concerns about moral hazard are set aside. For example, most central banks will be more tempted to relax limits on institutional participation in liquidity facilities when times are bad. That is perhaps odd as such facilities mostly serve as a backstop where they are only used under stressed scenarios anyway, but a crisis does focus minds differently. Risks are already crystallising on balance sheets at that stage, so the aim is no longer to avoid encouraging them to grow, but is instead there to minimise the costs of correction. The main difference between the facilities aimed at individual institutions and the more systemic ones tends to be the maturity of the funding. Whereas an organisation should only ever struggle for a short period during a bullish market, many businesses could struggle for longer periods during large cyclical downturns. By making funding available for a few years, banks receive some certainty that reduces the incentive for them to retrench aggressively.

Most liquidity facilities are provided by national central banks to ease problems in their currency area before they create solvency restrictions. However, finance is a global industry with many of its institutions carrying assets and liabilities in multiple currencies. This spread can create situations where banks in one country have difficulties getting the funding they need in other currencies, despite being solvent. Problems have been most prone to occur in US dollar funding, as market participants scramble to the relative safety of such assets during global turmoil. Starving non-US banks of dollar funding could cause significant problems for those institutions that could ripple across the real economy of other countries, and that would not be good for the US economy either. As such, a global network of foreign exchange swap lines has been developing. These facilities allow a central bank to borrow the currency of another central bank and provide it to domestic institutions struggling to access that funding elsewhere. The local central bank bears the counterparty risk with the institutions it lends to and is obliged to unwind the swap at the original exchange rate on a given date in the future, which neutralises the effect of foreign currency fluctuations.

Swap lines, like many domestic liquidity facilities, are not intended for regular use. They exist as backstops rather than to set the price of funding in normal circumstances, with markets instead clear to find their levels independently. When institution-specific or systemic stresses occur, though, the existence of liquidity facilities becomes highly relevant. They can essentially cap the price in a variety of markets and potential variations in the usage fees might be the only thing to cause movement until conditions normalise. This chapter's explanation of how bank balance sheets work and the rationale behind macroprudential policies will come into their own in such stressed scenarios. In more normal times, these things will be exerting smaller direct effects on the real economy. Overall, macroprudential policies are probably best thought of as trimming the tail risks ahead of and in the aftermath of significant cyclical shocks while monetary policy manages the central demand outlook for the next few years. Markets should price the full probability distribution, so both are potentially tradeable, although monetary policy remains king, as part 3 will explore.

Main Messages

- Banks must hold liquid assets ready for sale in the event of a temporary funding shortage. They must also hold their own capital to cover potential losses on their assets.
- When capital or liquidity requirements change, the bank can adjust to meet the target by changing either the asset or liability side of its balance sheet. The policymakers intended response need not be the one delivered, with potential costs for the real economy during adjustment.
- Banks are required to hold some capital at all times to avoid failure and its socialised costs. Beyond that, there are buffers designed for use during stressed periods. The capital conservation buffer (CCoB, 2.5%), countercyclical capital buffer (CCyB) and supervisor-set buffers for individual institutions are the buffers regulators intend to be used.
- Capital requirements used to focus on weighted risk assets, but desire to avoid underappreciated risks crystallising led to the non-risk-weighted leverage ratio. This measure is a simple backstop for constraining systemic risk.
- Intent to resell loans or to build market share for economies of scale could cause lending standards to loosen in a way that is optimal for a bank, at least in the short term, but bad for society overall. Regulated limits on lending standards can potentially prevent excessively lax standards.
- Excessive concentration of risk can cause systemic problems, perhaps by banks having too much exposure to borrowers over-stretching their income or overly leveraging their purchase. The need to accept price markdowns when selling repossessed assets can feed on itself as price falls weaken the market, begetting more possessions and price falls.
- Policymakers mostly subscribe to the doctrine of Walter Bagehot, which prescribes liquidity in abundance for solvent institutions. Potential losses are constrained by lending for a fee against collateral. Support can be provided to individual organisations or on a systemic basis that might crowd out the private market activity and determine the price of what is left.
- Macroprudential policies might typically be thought to trim tail risks ahead of and in the aftermath of shocks, while monetary policy is used to manage the central demand outlook.

Further Reading

Bank of England. 2015. *The Bank of England's approach to stress testing the UK banking system.*

Bank of England. 2015. *The Bank of England's Sterling Monetary Framework (the 'Red Book').*

European Commission. 2013. *Capital Requirements Directive.* Directive 2013/36/EU.

Basel Committee on Banking Supervision. 2011. *Basel III: A global regulatory framework for more resilient banks and banking systems.* Bank for International Settlements.

Part III

Financial Markets

While policymakers aim to improve outcomes, it is not always possible or desirable to interact with the real economy directly. So for monetary policy, in particular, financial markets are often used as the vehicle of choice. Details of capital movements are typically still deferred to market participants, who will ultimately profit from them. Doing so should aid the allocative efficiency of capital, at least in an economic sense, although the extent is subject to much ideological debate, as revealed through often widely different policy interventions. It is the profit motive that nonetheless ultimately drives a successful investor's response, whatever the source or sense of the shock. And it is the underlying economics that determines where prices should fundamentally find fair value. Not all of those economic factors may originate from the macroeconomy though. In fact, some of the most interesting will be emergent from the rational self-interest of many individuals. Market structure has a significant effect on the sometimes non-linear or even chaotic outcomes here. With regulatory changes turning structures on their head, it is now especially important to understand how this interacts with the real economy to drive movements in real markets.

This part begins with the plumbing of the financial system, which might at first seem too far away from the sexy trading topics you're ready to read here. However, this stuff is essential to market functioning. Understanding what money is, how it is created and how it interacts with capital underlie everything. Having got to grip with these concepts, we move on to the specific capital instruments. The concepts for fixed income, currency and commodity markets will be explored sequentially. Next, it's on to the other major asset class—i.e. equities. Economics is far more important here than you might think from reading the many research reports on this asset class. Derivatives exist for all of these in numerous varieties, where each can be tailored to express particular views, making them highly attractive for some investors. Finally, this part concludes with an examination of why and how we construct portfolios of these assets. An integral component of this is occasions when markets have amplified small shocks almost beyond recognition. Their nonconformity with standard models sometimes causes them to be ignored, but investors in real markets don't have that luxury, so they must be lashed to our robust framework too.

7
Financial Plumbing

Everyone knows what money is to them, but that may not be a good reflection of what it is in reality. Even seasoned economists and investors can become muddled over the important distinction between central bank and commercial bank money. The interaction between them is crucial to understanding the transmission of monetary policy into the equivalent rates effective in the economy. Without understanding this, operational changes cannot be anticipated, thereby causing any associated trades to be missed. These markets are relatively niche, though, so that might not be much of a concern. Exerting a much wider effect is the creation and destruction of money, which banks have the privilege of being able to do. Capital still needs to be issued to ensure the bank can cover plausible potential losses, so there is an unavoidable interaction with money. However, the securities issued to raise that capital have many uses in their own right, with more direct market consequences.

7.1 Money

There has been money for far longer than the existence of the medium most people consider to be money. In the modern sense, though, central banks are sitting at the centre of the financial market infrastructure. The central bank has a monopoly on banknotes, which are a liability of it, but far larger and more important are the reserves they issue. These become assets of commercial banks and are used to settle their transactions between each other.

P. Rush, *Real Market Economics*,
https://doi.org/10.1057/978-1-349-95278-6_7

These reserves are the water pumping through the plumbing of the financial system. How this central bank money translates into the wider economy is an important focus of this section. First, though, is an exploration of the crucial role that these reserves play in the payment systems facilitating all of our electronic transactions.

7.1.1 Payment Systems

For most people, it is enough to know that when they try to send some money to somebody, it will get there. The fact that problems are rare means the plumbing of the payments systems gets taken for granted, but that in no way kerbs how crucial it is to the economy. Without such plumbing, the population would be forced back to using inefficient and risky systems. Indeed, if money could not be sent electronically, we would be compelled to use physical cash as the exchange medium, or barter. That would be a huge constraint on economic activity. So, this relatively unglamorous part of the financial system can usually be ignored but never forgotten.

Those systems used most on a day-to-day basis—the "high-touch" ones—concern the provision of electronic payments, along with the withdrawal of physical cash. In many simple cases, the transaction starts and ends with the same bank, allowing the settlement to be fully resolved by the one bank. Even the difference in customer experience when sending money to another bank is relatively negligible nowadays. That is because central infrastructure is processing all these payments, including withdrawals of cash from an automated teller machine (from Vocalink in the UK). This infrastructure processes each transaction individually (i.e. gross) between member banks, which can then credit or debit their customers' accounts.

In modern economies, the money in the accounts of individuals and companies sits as commercial bank money, which is what is normally dealt with between banks, including for debit and credit card payments. But the flows ordered by banks' clients will not net out at all times, causing net obligations to accumulate that can only be eliminated by the transfer of an asset between the banks through a settlement agent Fig. 7.1. This agent could be a commercial bank, as is the case when they net out offsetting flows, but settlement can also use central bank money. An electronic transfer between reserves accounts at the central bank does exactly that. Ensuring this process occurs smoothly is a prerequisite for the smooth functioning of the payment systems. For systemically important payments, the central bank's negligible default risk makes it the natural settlement agent. It gains these credentials because of its monopoly licence to print money and the backstop provided

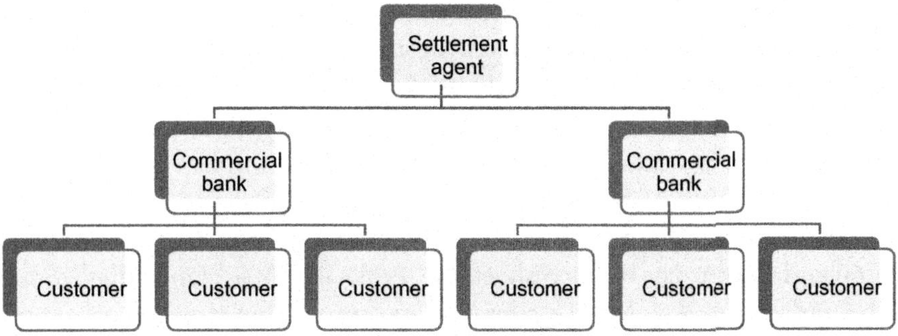

Fig. 7.1 The payment pyramid account structure

by the government. Settling the net obligations that arise between banks from the regular retail systems is suitably critical. Arguably more systemic are those for high-value securities and cash settlement systems (i.e. CREST and CHAPS in the UK), which need to settle immediately.

Settlement using central bank money is currently done in the UK using a real time gross settlement (RTGS) system. All payments processed by this are settled individually (gross, not net) and are irrevocable. The downside is that this is an inefficient use of liquidity because the full amount must be transferred with each instruction. This cost is probably offset by the removal of settlement risk associated with the unintended credit exposures that would otherwise build-up between the clearing cycles of a deferred net settlement (DNS) system. So RTGS uses central bank money to settle cash transfers within CHAPS and to pay for securities in CREST. Host to all the accounts in RTGS and carrying out all of their postings is the RTGS processor, within which sits the Central Scheduler used by CHAPS banks to control the rate and the order of their instructions proceeding to settlement. By dealing with non-urgent requests in delayed clearing cycles, liquidity efficiency can be boosted by up to 30% on some estimates. In doing so, the probability of running out of reserves reduces.

If settlement activity does demand more liquidity than held in reserves, the central bank can provide intra-day liquidity via same-day repos secured against collateral that is both highly liquid and high quality. An active decision may need to be taken to draw intra-day liquidity (e.g. for CHAPS), or it might be triggered automatically once a liquidity need is identified (e.g. if there are insufficient funds to settle a CREST transaction). Again, to reduce counterparty risk, loans are collateralised, which might be against the clearing securities or others already held. Through this mechanism, an Auto Collateralising Repo is provided, allowing the transaction to complete.

Funds cannot be delayed without breaking from the process of simultaneously delivering the security and transferring the cash. This so-called real-time Delivery versus Payment (DvP) settlement process adds valuable confidence to the system as all counterparties know they will not get left out of pocket from the other side of the transaction not completing.

A side effect of this additional intra-day liquidity provision is that the central bank's balance sheet gets boosted. For example, in mid-2012, the Bank of England's intra-day balance sheet was typically 15% higher than its size at the end of the day. With settlement accounts being the regular reserves accounts held by the Bank of England's counterparties, it is a rise in high-quality collateral and reserves that drive this intra-day increase on either side of the balance sheet. That is necessary because those reserves balances are the settlement asset for a variety of payment systems. Central bank reserves are the premier liquid asset because of their use as the ultimate settlement asset, which can be transferred irrevocably in real time. This quality places reserves in high demand, especially under the post-crisis regulatory system, which requires financial institutions to hold large liquid asset buffers.

7.1.2 Central Bank Money

Acquiring reserves is not merely a case of transferring some money into an account at the central bank, despite this being the way it is commonly discussed. Like banknotes, reserves are central bank money, and commercial bank money cannot turn into that without the central bank's involvement. They are liabilities of different entities. Reserves are a liability of the central bank, whereas commercial bank money is a liability of the issuing commercial bank. Banks have to place assets as collateral with the central bank for use in its operations to get central bank money outside of the settlement process. Those assets then counterbalance the additional liabilities from reserves creation, keeping the balance sheet necessarily balanced. Until quantitative easing became widespread, short-term open market operations were used to acquire the majority of assets, providing central bank money in exchange. Most of this central bank money took the form of banknotes. That is because the primary use of reserves was as a settlement asset, not a liquid asset, so commercial banks did not feel the need to hold large reserve balances at that time. Nowadays, banks do need to hold reserves as liquid assets for regulatory purposes, but the role of banknotes has not changed much.

The large-scale purchase of government bonds under quantitative easing programmes caused a considerable increase in the size of central bank balance sheets. In exchange for the bonds it was buying, the central banks credited the commercial bank selling it (directly or as an intermediary) with additional reserves. That creation of money is quantitative easing (QE), and it causes a surge in the stock of reserves, albeit not necessarily in line with the value of bonds bought outright, because it can crowd out other liquidity facilities. With QE determined by monetary policymakers, its decisions have become the primary driver of the stock of reserves. If a bank decides it wants more than the current elevated stock of reserves, most likely in response to a liquidity shock, there are still other options. Such policies were discussed in Chap. 6.

The stock of reserves held, and the variations caused by transactional requirements have another relationship with monetary policy that is even more relevant to financial markets. Chapter 5 explored the aims and transmission of monetary policy, but not how the policy rate relates to other interest rates in the real economy. After all, banking in most countries is a private sector activity that is competitive, even when banks might be nationalised in the interests of financial stability, so it's not like the policy announcement is just an unavoidable direction to them. Banks pass on changes in the policy rate to the deposit and lending rates that they offer because that is the profitable thing to do. If another bank is offering a higher interest rate, customer deposits will flow to it, with a movement in central bank reserves occurring to facilitate the settlement. Where those reserves are remunerated at the central bank, there is a loss of interest income. If that lost revenue exceeds the cost of paying the customer, after adjusting for balance sheet costs, the bank will have lost out. It is thereby encouraged to raise its deposit rate towards the policy rate because its profits maximise where marginal revenues equal marginal costs. This optimisation should naturally cause a convergence of interest rates around the policy rate while encouraging the transmission of changes to the degree that it is profitable to do so.

When the balance sheet cost is high, perhaps because of a shortage of capital, banks may need to see vast differences in interest rates before it becomes profitable for them to change their pricing. Such deviations weaken the implementation of monetary policy. For policymakers to control interest rates with the aim of achieving their target, it can help to encourage banks to transact with each other. Encouragement can be given through the requirement to average a targeted stock of reserves over a specified period, typically between monetary policy decisions. This arrangement is a reserve averaging framework. If the settlement of transactions causes a drift away from that target, the bank will need to borrow or lend elsewhere so that its reserves balance can settle back into the required range. Because the central bank controls the total level of reserves, it can ensure that if one bank is above target, another is below it by the same amount, so there should be some interest elsewhere to transact.

An active market in interbank lending is not always enough to keep effective rates linked to the policy rate, but without this need, banks may not maintain the in-house capabilities to transact in this way. Profitable arbitrage trades can then be missed because no one is watching for them, thereby allowing effective rates to drift. It's a bit like driving down a bumpy road without any hands on the wheel. When the system is facing demands for reserves that are very different from the prevailing supply, an active interbank market is still not going to keep rates near the policy one. There will just be lots of activity near a different rate. In the interests of maintaining monetary control, it can be desirable to bound how far effective rates can deviate away from the intended policy setting. Providing operational standing facilities that will absorb or provide unlimited reserves at a specified deposit or lending rate serves this purpose. While wholesale interest rates remain within that corridor, there is no incentive to use these facilities because it is cheaper to transact in the market. But pressures beyond that are bounded by the ability of the central bank to stand in the middle with these facilities and disintermediate the financial market.

If the stock of reserves became insufficient to meet the collective liquidity needs of banks, attempts to borrow in the market would cause rates to rise above the policy rate. But when the overnight rate reaches the marginal lending facility rate, the central bank will be willing to lend instead and there is little incentive to look to other banks anymore. In practice, a systemic shock would probably see other more generous liquidity schemes kick in first, though. On the other side, there could be a surplus supply of reserves, perhaps because of their excess creation during quantitative easing. The desire to offload the excess would cause attempts to lend them out at lower interest rates, but only as far as the deposit rate Fig. 7.2. At that point, banks are better off holding them and receiving that income instead of lending out and earning less from another bank. Shifts in the balance between supply and demand of reserves can, therefore, cause drifts within the corridor of policy rates, which can be extreme enough to cause one bound to become the effective policy rate. Sometimes the central bank might change policy to discourage this, like remunerating all reserves at the central policy rate, regardless of how many a bank holds, or varying the corridor's width or skew. There is lots of room to control monetary policy's implementation here. It is mostly left to those without a central bank reserve account to cause the remaining problems, which can be curtailed naturally by extending such access.

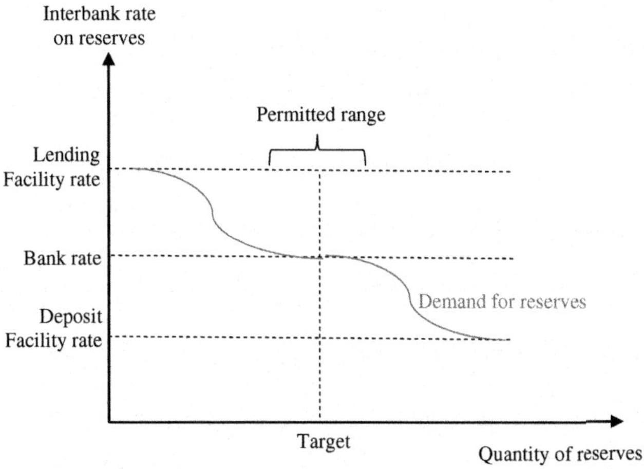

Fig. 7.2 Policy interest rate corridor

Another way to control a drift below the policy rate is to sterilise the excess of reserves. Offering a term deposit facility is one option, which will drain a number of liquid reserves. Issuance of central bank bonds is the other way to achieve this, as purchases of these bonds from the central bank will settle in exchange for reserve balances that self-destruct in the process. The central bank is just transforming its liabilities from reserves to bonds, which have different characteristics. These bonds can trade in secondary markets, where all manner of investors can buy them. Those without reserve accounts at the central bank can then buy these instead of lending cash elsewhere overnight at rates below the policy rate. These bonds might also be offered at longer terms. One difficulty is knowing how many to issue. The central bank could make an educated guess of how many reserves it needs to sterilise and issue accordingly. Alternatively, it could ask banks to set their preferred target level of reserves. Everything beyond that self-identified level of demand would be an excess, which could be sterilised by the issuance of central bank bonds.

7.2 Making Money

Aiding the central bank's control over its liabilities is its special status as an insolvency-proof institution. It can create as many reserves as it likes and no one will doubt its ability to pay. The only risk is inflation eroding the value, which would also affect every other conventional fixed income asset (i.e.

some are inflation-linked). Counterparty credit risk is not something that would push investors away from holding liabilities of the central bank even if they were to increase tenfold. This robust demand gives the central bank unlimited room to increase its supply of money through policies like quantitative easing. Where assets are bought from commercial banks, there is just a transformation in the type of asset it holds, from the asset that the central bank has bought to what the central bank offers in return. However, when the asset comes from another investor, the commercial bank will credit the original holder's bank account with money. This deposit is not technically the same central bank money that the commercial bank will have received for facilitating the transaction, although they are related. The commercial bank money is a newly created liability of the commercial bank, which balances the reserves asset it received from the central bank. New money can, therefore, be created in the wider economy during QE. However, most money is not created this way. Commercial banks have the power to create their own money independently of what the central bank is doing.

7.2.1 Fractional Reserve Banking

Perceptions about money can be wildly different from reality. When someone deposits money in a bank, they can see that that amount raises their account value and it is available to withdraw whenever they want. That is all true, but the temptation to believe that the money is always sitting there with the depositor's name on it waiting for withdrawal is not. There is no hard asset behind each unit of currency that fixes the amount in circulation. Commercial banks are instead allowed to perform a useful confidence trick that can benefit society. That has mostly been the case for hundreds of years.

Once upon a time, people used to exchange gold or other precious metals when transacting. It was durable, divisible and of consistently high value to make it widely desirable to hold. These qualities made it a good medium of exchange, but it was also bulky and dangerous to carry around. So, people would deposit it with goldsmiths for safe keeping. The goldsmith would need to charge the depositor for that service and in return, provide a receipt acknowledging that they owe the bearer some gold. As the renown of these goldsmiths grew, receipts became recognised and accepted in their own right. They were a convenient alternative to transferring gold without the need to withdraw and re-deposit it. A form of paper money is born, with a commitment to pay the bearer the stated value in gold. This paper is great for simple transactional purposes, but not much help for people needing to borrow money. If the goldsmith always had to hold on to that gold for the bearer of the promissory note, their ability to lend would be constrained by the capital built up from retained earnings. Borrowing would be hard to find and accordingly expensive, thereby starving potentially productive investments of the needed resources.

The significant change is to permit goldsmiths to lend out the depositor's gold by writing additional promissory notes on the same deposit. Gold still backs each note, but there is no longer enough gold to cover all of the claims on it. Only a fractional reserve exists. With goldsmiths able to write many notes on the same deposit, their ability to lend money significantly increases. Borrowers will find it much easier and cheaper to fund their investment projects by extension. And because the initial deposit gains a value to the goldsmith beyond a potential income from selling its warehoused safety, there is an incentive to offer much more generous terms to depositors. The spread between borrowing and lending rates reduces, and everyone will be happy. Or at least they will be provided that the goldsmith doesn't get too greedy and write too many promissory notes. Doing so would raise their interest income but at the increased risk of not having enough gold on hand to pay back those who might legitimately call in those promises to pay back that gold.

Nowadays there is a central bank with the sole right to issue notes, and it is rare for the promises made on those notes to be convertible back into gold. This monopoly has the advantage of avoiding notes from unscrupulous people circulating and harming the acceptability of other respectable notes. When there is a single legal tender everyone in the economy knows that the money they hold will be acceptable to everyone they might wish to transact with at a price written on the note. No risk adjustment is needed between notes when they all have the same issuer. And so long as a modern bank is widely seen to be safe, people will be happy to leave their money within them knowing that the balance listed in their account is available when they need it. If that confidence disappears, depositors will naturally want to make sure they get their money out first because they know that the bank doesn't have enough money to pay back all the depositors it owes. The anticipation of a bank run is enough to cause one. All banks rely on the confidence trick that deposits are available for everyone who sees that money in the account and any bank will die if that confidence is lost.

Banks are clearly in a privileged position to literally make money. When a bank writes a new loan, this will normally occur without raising any additional funds. All it needs to do is credit the account of the new borrower with some money, which it has created. The bank's balance sheet will expand with the loan on the asset side and the new deposit as its liability, while the opposite applies to the borrower. Because it is new money, no other depositors will see their account balance fall because of this, although a smaller portion of the deposit will now be reserved in case of a run. If fewer borrowers wish to borrow from the bank, this process works in reverse, with deposits paid back to the bank in return for the loan balance shrinking. Such repayments are how money dies. Capital needs to be held against the risks of loss on all outstanding loans, but this capital is raised at discrete intervals rather than typically binding lending behaviours. Capital has other relationships with money too, and its own complexities to consider within the plumbing of the financial system.

7.2.2 Capital

When a bank sells some shares in itself, it is exchanging equity capital for cash, where the latter is liquid funds that can potentially be reinvested in an expansion of the balance sheet. Selling a bond of some sort instead adds both an asset (cash) and a liability (bond) to the issuing bank's balance sheet. For the investor, there is just an exchange of assets (cash for bond) but there are more assets around overall. An increased supply of financial assets would depress market prices if all else is equal and on some new issue days this depressing effect can be apparent. On others, though, the supply effectively creates its own demand as the system generates an increased money supply to absorb the issue. Because the money supply can be increased by the activities of central and commercial banks, there is not a fixed volume of financial wealth to divide up between securities. The metaphorical pie can grow as well as be divided up differently. Investing is not a zero-sum game in the sense that sometimes everyone will win or lose, albeit by different amounts.

Financial market participants facilitate the growth in capital values through the use of repurchase agreements (repos). Central banks use these with banks to collateralise the loans it makes to them in the various liquidity facilities on offer. On these occasions, possession of the financial assets is taken by the central bank while the ownership remains with the bank, unlike when they buy assets outright under quantitative easing programmes. Through the creation of new central bank money, the overall money supply is increased to finance the existence of that asset. Such repos are usually only overnight but might be for longer periods or regularly rolled over. To the extent that the central bank's balance sheet maintains a higher overall size dedicated to repos, financial asset prices will be supported, similar to when the assets are bought outright. This relative inflationary impulse might not be desirable for the deliverance of monetary policy objectives, but that is why the availability and generosity of such schemes are controlled.

Repos also regularly occur without any central bank involvement, albeit with different terms. Between private parties, repos are normally structured as sale and repurchase agreements, where the *ownership* is transferred too, rather than just the possession under repos that merely collateralise a loan. In a sale and repurchase repo, the borrower temporarily sells the asset and receives cash while promising to repurchase the asset in future at a specified price. Built into that price is the interest due by the borrower, where the repo rate is the annualised interest rate on the transaction. This interest rate will depend on the expected total return on the asset and also the scarcity of it. Money market funds tend to be large cash providers under repos as they value the security of the loan, its flexibility and the yield uplift it can offer them. On the other side of the transaction are often banks and hedge funds that have taken positions, perhaps temporarily, and need to finance them. Where a bank is receiving cash in this way, it is potentially able to leverage that fractional reserve up, thereby increasing the overall supply of money.

Riskier assets require a larger haircut to be built into the price, and this is one source of highly non-linear distributions of asset price changes. When something causes market participants to increase the perceived risk of an asset, cash providers will demand a greater rate of return for participating in the repo. With a larger haircut priced into a given asset, less money can be raised from its repo. When that money has been leveraged up as a fractional reserve, its loss can cause for a much larger pool of loans to lose their funding. Either new money needs to be raised via other means or the stock of lending needs to be reduced. A more widespread loss of asset values can occur under the latter scenario, which increases risks and the repo haircuts even more. Shocks are thereby magnified through bank leverage and their use of repos to receive cash. And where a shock is also a function of itself, it is inherently non-linear. The distribution of returns will contain much fatter tails than the normal distribution as a result, contrary to the standard assumptions of portfolio theory.

An additional complication comes from the potential for an asset to be used multiple times in a repo. For example, someone who expects interest rates to rise might lend cash to receive a bond on a term repo and then lend that same bond out on rolling overnight repos. If interest rates increase, the money earned on those overnight loans shall rise, and if the degree was more than the market had initially priced, the overall receipts would exceed the amount due back at the end. That would be a profitable trade, but it relies on having the collateral available to both borrow and lend on again. This process is known as re-hypothecation, and it is a crucial mechanism for leveraging securities. If an asset is bought by an investor who won't lend it out again, the room for leverage reduces. When a central bank requires asset placements as collateral for a repo with it, the asset becomes encumbered by that claim on it. In limited quantities that is fine, but when systemic support is provided and there is a concentration of the assets used as collateral, this encumbrance risks impeding market functioning. Concerns that stimulus might have negative side effects without proper management is one motivation for policymakers accepting a broad range of collateral in its operations. And when government bonds are bought outright, there are often arrangements for some of them to be available for on-lending to the market via repos, thereby preventing painful and unnecessary squeezes associated with asset shortages. Capital's relationship with money means it cannot be ignored even when the policy is implemented with entirely different matters in mind.

Main Messages

- Banknotes and reserve balances are liabilities of the central bank whereas the deposits held electronically at banks are their liabilities instead. Central banks control their liabilities, not commercial banks, although the latter's requirements will influence provision.
- Payments might net out within a bank, but there is a natural need for net transfers to be made between banks. Typically used to settle transactions are reserve balances at the central bank.
- Banks pass on changes in the policy rate to their deposit and lending rates that they offer when that is the profitable thing to do—i.e. the marginal revenue exceeds the marginal cost.
- Operational standing facilities can provide extensive deposits or lending at penal rates, thereby putting limits on where market rates can drift relative to the policy rate. When there is a significant imbalance in supply and demand for reserves balances, the effective policy rate might become another rate defined in the operational corridor.
- Offering a term deposit facility or converting reserves into bonds can sterilise an excess supply of reserves and the associated effect it has on market rates.
- Deposits placed with a bank are not set aside for that depositor and are instead lent out to others. Money is created in the process. With multiple claims on the same money, there is a fractional reserve banking system that beneficially makes loans more available and deposits remunerative.

- If confidence is lost in a bank's ability to pay its depositors, a bank run will occur. No bank can simultaneously repay all its creditors.
- Sale and repurchase agreements (repos) allow finance to be raised on capital. When the value of that capital falls, less funding can be raised, thereby further reducing asset prices. By feeding on itself, this is one recipe for non-linear distributions in asset price changes.
- Securities can be leveraged through repos by reusing the collateral, which is known as re-hypothecation.
- Some central bank claims can cause encumbrance of collateral that restricts funding room. Facilities to remake some of those assets available exist to avoid unnecessary squeezes that otherwise harm financial market functioning.

Further Reading

Bank of England. 2013. *A Guide to the Bank of England's Real Time Gross Settlement System.*

Bank of England. 2013. *Bank of England Settlement Accounts.*

Bank of England. 2014. *Documentation for the Bank of England's operations under the sterling monetary framework.*

Norman, Ben. Shaw, Rachel. Speight, George. 2011. *The history of interbank settlement arrangements: exploring central banks' role in the payment system.* BoE Working Paper No. 412.

8
The Markets

It is finally time to apply the economic framework to real markets directly. Naturally, this means focussing on the fundamental factors driving financial prices, although this is not the only thing that will affect actual performance. Most traders will also watch technical factors for guides as to what pricing patterns are likely to emerge. Some treat technical analysis as a mystic art where even outlandish indicators become runes to read. Correlation can be confused for causality in egregious data mining exercises spuriously back fitting recent price moves. It shouldn't come as a surprise to hear an economist scoff at such things, but when enough of the market is looking at the same levels to buy or sell it; those technical factors can nonetheless be self-fulfilling. And how those technical levels are defended can tell you a lot about the appetite of active market participants to put on trades in one direction or the other.

Many of the best macrotraders will time when they enter their fundamental positions by referring to simple technical factors like turning points around recent trends, reversal proportions of previous moves or moving averages of price action (including crossovers of moving averages with different look back periods). More complicated measures, like the "Ichimoku Cloud", can also sometimes work in niche markets where that become known as a thing to watch. Nor is there just one horizon to apply such technical indicators over. It might be fitting to overlay some to an intraday chart while other levels might have relevance for months or even years. Market

P. Rush, *Real Market Economics*,
https://doi.org/10.1057/978-1-349-95278-6_8

price dynamics are not obviously different when you zoom out of a graph, which is why some people talk fondly of fractals. When longer-lived resistance levels approach, there can be a spike in volatility as it breaks or is retracted from, so some traders like to place derivative trades around such technical events. Breaks of technical resistance can also provide a sign that there is an appetite among market participants to enter new fundamental positions.

Fundamentally speaking, financial market prices are a combination of the expected return value and the risk premium demanded by investors for the exchange. What this means in practice will depend on the underlying asset. Fixed income, currencies and commodities (FICC) trade on macrofactors and tend to be grouped within banks, but they are very different from each other. Like equities, fixed income securities are capital assets in the sense that they are priced as the net present value of discounted future cash flows. In this case, the issuer is committed to paying coupons under a predetermined formula, culminating in the return of the principal amount at maturity. Commodities and currencies don't neatly fit this definition. Currency is better thought of as a store of value because it is neither directly consumable nor yielding of cash flow, but it can be exchanged for things that are either. Commodities are different again because they are for consumption or transfer, and so have an economic value rather than a set of cash flows. Equities distinguish themselves by offering an asset with no maturity and a series of uncertain cash flows to the price that will be determined by many microeconomic factors too. Financial derivatives exist for FICC and equities, and exploration of this area will round-off this important chapter.

8.1 Fixed Income

There are many types of fixed income securities, each with a different type of underlying exposure. Those with the shortest maturities can be considered close to cash and are known as money market instruments, while bonds are issued with longer maturities. Groups of assets can also be pooled together into a new securitized product that is both more liquid and diversified. Some issuers will use each of these pools. Governments mostly issue Bonds and Bills, but might also securitize other assets like its book of student loans. Corporates can similarly issue Bonds and Commercial Paper. Banks are usually involved in any issuance from other sectors, but will also issue Bonds, a variety of securitised products and certificates of deposit (Fig. 8.1).

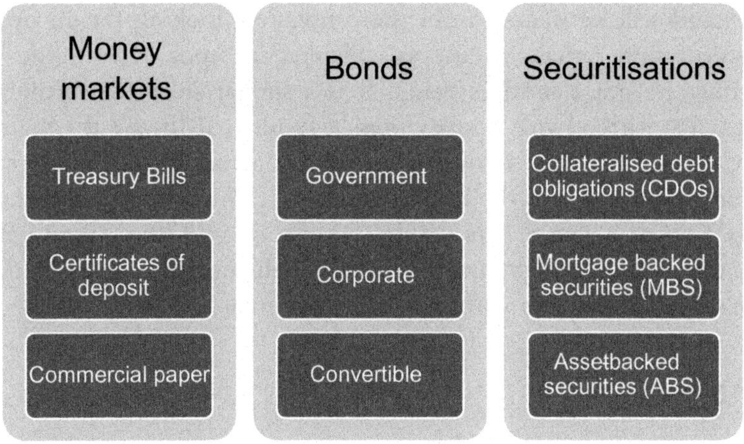

Fig. 8.1 Fixed income markets

8.1.1 Money Markets

Within money markets, governments are large issuers. Most Bills are issued with a three-month maturity, although there are some with six- or twelve-month maturities too. Because of their short lifespan, the only cash flows tend to be the initial loan and the repayment at the end of the term. Compensation for the loan comes from the difference between the issuance and redemption prices, which creates the discount rate. Governments vary the stock of Bills in issue during the year because their cash flows are similarly variable. When the expected cash requirement changes during the year, it is sometimes advisable to amend the stock of Bill issuance rather than changing bond issuance programmes or fiscal policy.

It is anyway important to maintain some portion of government debt in Bills. Doing so keeps market participants engaged ahead of any changes in issuance. These Bills are also about as close to risk-free as it comes, so they are prized for use in the repurchase agreements that help sustain the smooth functioning of financial markets. Defaulting on these could be extremely damaging, but this is rarely driving price changes. Monetary policy tends to provide the anchor for the discount rate, sometimes explicitly when the central bank is itself issuing Bills to sterilise the stock of reserves. Supply of Bills relative to the demand for them in repos, or as safe liquid assets will then determine the tradeable price around that policy anchor.

Corporates issue Bills too with similar terms, but their commercial paper (CP) is inherently riskier, and it trades differently as a result. Monetary policy remains the anchor, but supply from any issuer will be relatively small, and demand will be mainly from those investors looking for an uplift on cash returns rather than for use as collateral in repos or as liquid assets, which they are not classed as being. It is a similar story for certificates of deposit (CD) with a bank. Money market funds (MMF) are the main buyers of CP and CD because they can diversify across issuers and provide a more consistent return to the investors placing cash with them. Unlike term deposits with or between banks, CD can also be sold like CP and Bills in the secondary market if the investor wants their money back early, perhaps because someone wants to withdraw money from an MMF.

8.1.2 Bonds

Bonds are issued with longer terms until they mature (including some perpetual issues, which never do), and because waiting decades for a return is unattractive when a default might happen in the interim, bonds issue with regularly scheduled interest payments. These payments occur once or twice a year and are known as coupons since old bearer bonds had physical tickets to tear off when claiming the interest. Pricing at first issue typically sets the bond at a similar price to the nominal value a conventional bond would redeem at, so the prevailing interest rates will determine the coupon rate at the time of issue. As a market rates inevitable change, the bond will trade above or below its par value, thereby, respectively, adding negative or positive yield from holding the bond to maturity. The coupon yield and annualised percentage difference from the redemption value together represent the overall yield to maturity. Inflation-linked bonds have the additional complication of the redemption value being upscaled in line with a price index, thereby allowing it to maintain its real value.

A yield curve formed of all the outstanding bonds might look relatively smooth, but that does not mean that prices will respond in an obviously proportionate way as the yield to maturity changes. Potentially significant differences in prevailing interest rates at the time of issue means that there is variation in the coupon rate between bonds. Bonds with high coupons will be paying out more of their value at earlier periods, so the traded price will be less sensitive to changes in yield than one with low coupons and back-loaded income. This effect is recorded by a bond's duration, which is intuitively the average time to receive all the cash flows. Duration is necessarily lower than maturity because some of those cash flows are paid ahead of redemption as coupons. If there's a lower coupon, more of the cash flow will come from the bond's redemption, so the average time to receive the cash flows will be longer and the duration higher. As a given change in yield will affect those longer-dated cash flows by more, the price of this low-coupon bond will vary by more than a high coupon one. And because inflation-linked bonds have low coupons relative to the uplifted redemption values, they will have far higher duration than the equivalent conventional bond.

Duration is measured in years and is informative, but it can translate into more useful forms. Modified duration measures the approximate change in bond price for a 1% change in yield. Alternatively, the dollar value of a basis point (DV01) expresses this in hard currency terms and is a favoured risk measure for many rates traders. All are acceptable when talking about small changes in yield, but are not when large changes occur. Duration is technically a first-order approximation that will underestimate the price change associated with a given yield change. Adjusting for the error requires the curvature of the present value/yield profile to be modelled, which is done using convexity as a second-order measure of interest rate risk. It is the rate price variation to yield varies with respect to yield. Bond convexity is a positive function of cash-flow dispersion and duration. If you need any of these measures, bond data providers typically list them, or you can use one of the many calculators or functions that are publicly available.

Interest rate levels will move in response to changes in either the expected path for monetary policy or term premium. When the central bank is expected to tighten, the curve will be upward sloping, while loosening expectations lead to an inverted curve. The latter can be painful for banks, which borrow short and lend long, so such a curve shape can bring about recessionary pressures as well as be a warning sign. Kinks in the curve can also occur when policy mistakes are expected. Hiking too slowly means that the policy rate will need to overshoot the neutral rate temporarily to bring it back down. Meanwhile, term premium is the additional compensation investors demand for holding long duration assets. Concerns about the credit quality of the issuer or the liquidity of the security can affect the term premium. Investors' inherent preferences can also create kinks in the term structure, perhaps because they value long duration bonds to match their liabilities, leaving an unloved part of the curve in the belly. When a central bank directly buys bonds, it also tends to compress term premium, with unloved sections of the curve moving most.

As expectations for the policy rate outlook evolve, the curve shape will respond progressively. When a tightening cycle begins to be anticipated, bonds will sell off and trade at higher yields, with the 10-year part of the curve usually underperforming shorter maturities. This move steepens up the shorter end of the curve and flattens it out beyond. Bullish expectations are raising the neutral rate and the path for policy to get there, but the former will only go so far. Yields at progressively shorter maturities should flatten as the cycle is priced in and ultimately delivered upon, assuming that occurs. If there is no follow through for policy, pricing in of new-found pessimism can cause a bullish flattening to roll out the curve, like an iron pushing toward longer maturities. When an adverse shock abruptly hits, the reduction in real yields and potentially inflation expectations can cause yields to decline, but monetary policy anchors the very short end. A damaging inversion of the yield curve can occur until either the central bank follows through with lower rates or the market changes its mind. Loosening cycles are almost always going to happen much quicker and in larger incremental changes than in hiking cycles.

Corporate bond yields are heavily influenced by the borrowing costs of the relevant sovereign for the currency in issue. Beyond that cost, though, the reduced liquidity of corporate paper and the increased default risk raise the yields required by investors to hold the bonds of one company relative to another or the government. That default risk is also divisible into the probability of default and the loss-given default. If a company has liquidity issues but a high book value that makes creditors likely to be repaid upon liquidation, it might not require as much of a discount on its bonds as a company with better cash flow but a terrible balance sheet position. Some bonds are classed as convertibles because they might turn into equity under particular adverse circumstances. For example, banks have been encouraged to issue contingent convertible bonds ("CoCos"), which will convert into equity when key capital ratios are falling too low, thereby allowing it to automatically shore up its balance sheet without tapping an equity market that is likely to be fragile in that environment.

8.1.3 Securitised Products

Pools of debt can be combined to provide the investor with diversification across a range of issues. The resultant bonds should, therefore, be less susceptible to idiosyncratic shocks, which reduces the risk profile and risk-adjusted returns by extension. This repackaging process into a new security is called securitisation, and it is attractive to many investors, despite the bad reputation it earned during the credit crunch. It doesn't help that plenty of people proclaim their bafflement rather than spending a few minutes learning what the acronyms mean. A collateralised debt obligation (CDO) is a security that provides a cash flow from a pool of debts serving as collateral for it, while a CDO squared is just a CDO of CDOs. An investor is taking a smaller portion of each borrower's risk as the underlying pool grows, thereby taking them closer to holding the "market" for such assets, not unlike what an MMF does for its investors. Mortgage-backed securities (MBS) work under the same principle but with mortgages where there is the additional risk of prepayments to price. Asset-backed securities (ABS) are the same sort of thing again, except that the underlying securities backing it are other receivables, like car loans, student loans, royalties or indeed any series of cash flows that can be packaged together.

Prepayment risk is special in the sense that it changes the duration of the security. If more loans are expected to be repaid early, or earlier, the average time to receive those cash flows shortens and so the duration does too by definition. This shortening or the opposite can occur because of changes in the economy or monetary policy. When the central bank reduces rates, loans can be financed cheaper, so it makes sense to repay the old loan early. Sometimes the change in duration will be offset by so-called convexity hedging, which involves buying (or selling) long-term bonds to maintain the same overall duration. This hedging activity has become far less prevalent in recent years, though, partly because central banks hold these assets for monetary policy purposes and they don't convexity hedge. Their provision of other funding sources that are relatively generous also means securitisation is less attractive nowadays. Some investors became disillusioned when they saw weak risk assessment on loans designed for securitisation lead to losses. Many investors remain interested when they understand that these securities reflect systemic risk in that market, rather than no risk, and when they are happy, lending standards are suitably strong. Breaking down each securitisation into multiple risk tranches, wherein losses from the underlying pool are differently concentrated, also allows investors to match their risk tolerance and view better than would otherwise be the case.

8.2 Currencies

The foreign exchange (FX) value of a currency is a particular focus of macroinvestors, many of whom will also trade fixed income. There are some important theoretical and practical relationships between such investments that make it possible to express some views, either way, especially using derivatives of them. Nonetheless, FX is often considered to be the dumb cousin, despite it necessarily involves more than one country, unlike with bonds. Relatively poor-quality models with weak fundamental anchors mean it can wander in unanticipated ways, with nonsensical analysis sometimes offered up as reasoning. Expressing and analysing opinions relative to a basket of currencies can help sterilise the potential for surprise in one to overwhelm an economic view on another. Overall, though, there are two main arbitrage conditions and a variety of behavioural factors that can be offered up.

8.2.1 Arbitrage Conditions

Uncovered interest parity (UIP) is arguably the most important arbitrage relationship, despite its poor reflection of reality. The assumption in UIP is that the exchange rate will move to equalise the relative risk-adjusted return between countries. When prevailing interest rates in one country are much higher than in another, the exchange rate is assumed to depreciate and vice versa. Many central banks and other relatively academic forecasters assume that UIP holds with their forecast. Doing so avoids making a call on the currency that risks seeming like guidance for a non-policy instrument, but it is also arguably better than just assuming no change.

Many market participants trade the explicit view that UIP doesn't hold. By buying a high yielding currency with a low-yielding one, the investor can potentially receive a favourable yield differential. This practice is called a carry trade. If UIP held, the investor would lose an equivalent amount through an FX move, but that tends not to be true. When risk appetite is high, investors tend to put carry trades on, bidding up the price of high-yielding currencies in the process. Adverse shocks can cause investors to lose their nerve such that they unwind carry trades, depressing the high-yielding currency in the process. Execution of carry trades means that even when UIP may appear to have been broadly held over a given period, the path between points will not have been a smooth glide.

The other main arbitrage condition is from purchasing power parity (PPP), which provides a theoretical anchor for the level of the exchange rate while UIP explains only the adjustment path. PPP assumes that prices should be the same between countries when they are expressed in a common currency. Price deviations should shift demand to the cheaper country, raising the real exchange rate of that country in the process. PPP is, therefore, akin to saying that there is a constant real effective exchange rate (REER) in the long run. However, transaction costs, differences in consumer preferences, a comparative advantage in production and heterogeneous exports mean that there isn't a hard and exploitable trade-off here in practice. To the extent that there is convergence in a currency to its equilibrium PPP level, it is likely to occur over many years and exert a negligible effect on the exchange rate at most times in the interim.

8.2.2 FX Models

Introducing flexibility in the modelled equilibrium exchange rate requires moving beyond the arbitrage conditions into more empirical models. Probably the most popular are behavioural equilibrium exchange rate (BEER) models. The main variables that have been identified and incorporated into BEER variations involve the terms of trade, net foreign assets, relative fiscal policy and productivity. The terms of trade can be expressed as the ratio of export to import prices, with some economists preferring to narrow it down to a select group of primary commodities. Net foreign assets are normalised either relative to total trade, GDP or GNP. Fiscal policy can be incorporated via numerous approaches, like the ratio of government consumption, deficit or debt to GDP. Productivity, in this case, is about the relative price of traded to non-traded goods, which might be proxied by the ratio of consumer to producer prices. All variables should be viewed relative to other countries.

The rationale for including the terms of trade is that a rise in the value of a country's exports acts as a positive wealth effect, attracting more inflows and pressure to appreciate. Net foreign assets should also have a positive relationship since a trade surplus is more beneficial to debtor countries that must service external liabilities, and a weaker exchange rate would help that. Meanwhile, government consumption supports the currency by raising demand in relatively non-tradeable areas and funding any related deficits and the stock of debt through bonds that foreign investors find attractive with a lower risk premium. Finally, upward pressure on the currency from relative productivity gains is normally attributed to the Balassa–Samuelson effect. Higher productivity in the tradable sector should put upward pressure on wages in the non-tradable sector, which results in a higher relative price of non-tradables and a real appreciation. Or with a simple carry-trading mindset, improved productivity raises real revenue growth, thereby making investments in that country a more attractive proposition.

Similar variables often feature in underlying balance models, which treat the real exchange rate as a relative price that must move to bring supply and demand into equilibrium. That does not mean full stock-flow equilibrium, but it does require the balance of savings and investment to seem sustainable, and the current account by extension. These kinds of models do not say anything about the way that an economy returns to equilibrium, not least because of they abstract from the important short-term pricing considerations. However, they do provide an interesting guide to the effect that certain structural shifts might have on the equilibrium exchange rate.

This guide is provided by estimating the structural equations for net trade and balance of interest, profit and dividend relationships, then inverting the model, so the real exchange rate is expressed in terms of the fundamental variables. Such estimates tend to be called the fundamental equilibrium exchange rate (FEER) as a result. The FEER is not the equilibrium level at all times, though, since it also relies upon internal balance being achieved, with demand equal to supply.

An alternative approach to analysing movements in FX over much shorter horizons is provided by financial fair value (FFV) models. These models estimate the historical relationship between changes in FX and the price of other asset classes. In doing so, another perspective is provided on what is driving the FX market at that time, while creating a short-term measure of fair value. The key assumption here is that exchange rates and asset prices are co-determined with relatively stable short-term relationships, so when there is a divergence between relative returns, there should be some payback. That doesn't mean that it is necessarily the currency that is mispriced, as corrections could come elsewhere, but estimates of the misalignment tend to close quicker than deviations from any of the other equilibrium concepts. FFV models can be especially useful during periods of central bank intervention, as their large order size can be disruptive to areas that temporarily disrupt the normal co-determination of asset prices.

8.3 Commodities

Some people don't see commodities as investments partly because they generate no cash flow. Commodities are real assets with an intrinsic use for consumption or investment. Other people find those qualities more attractive as monetary inflation does not diminish the real value of commodities, which are secured by their end use. That does not mean they have stable prices, though, with some typically trading with much higher volatility than more conventional asset classes. Nonetheless, their distinctive qualities mean that commodities can provide some diversification benefits to a portfolio and increase risk-adjusted returns, so they are normally seen as financial investments too. In practice, most investors will buy them using derivatives, which are discussed at the end of this chapter, or via their equity holdings of companies in this sector. As equities, there are many other idiosyncrasies to consider, though, as will be explored in the next section. The current focus is on the physical markets and the economics driving price movements.

8.3.1 Soft and Hard

Commodity markets divide into hard and soft ones, where the latter are perishable. Supply is significantly affected by the inability to store such goods for long periods as a failure for them to be consumed quickly enough will lead to wastage. There is often a seasonal pattern to the supply of such commodities, like livestock, grains and seeds, coffee, sugar, textiles and timber. Seasonality means supply is unusually fixed in the short term, despite it being highly variable in the long run. This time-variability of supply creates unusual price dynamics, sometimes called hog cycles. For example, when prices are high, farmers are encouraged to breed more pigs because the marginal revenue from doing so is expected to stay above the marginal cost until a higher level of sales. The next year, many farmers might see that their competitors did the same such that there is now a large supply overhang that crushes prices. Supply is encouraged to fall again, leading to another high-price, short-term equilibrium. The supply response might also be compounded by farmers withholding animals from slaughter to breed when the price is high and vice versa when it's low.

Adaptive expectations can create these cycles between locally stable high and low-price regimes, with low and high supply, respectively. The use of futures to lock in prices early and inertia to farmers' expectations means that cycles tend to be longer-lived than annual oscillations. Nonetheless, the supply of these real assets is subject to the same sort of deliberations that companies must go through, based on the microeconomic foundations of profit maximisation. Demand for most soft commodities also has a degree of seasonality, cyclicality and a trend. Some foods or garments are requested more at certain times of the year. Cyclical strength can raise demand for relatively expensive options as they appear more affordable. It is the same story underlying some trends too, with the citizens of developing countries changing their diets as wealth rises. Macroeconomic forecasts of demand for these soft commodities will need to include the cyclical and trends factors as well, while gaps relative to forecast supply imply pricing pressures.

Consumption is not the only use for commodities, even of the "soft" kind. Timber has numerous applications in construction, especially of residential properties. That means demand for wood will be linked to new housing starts, which are in turn driven by the financial activities of households. Growth in real incomes and employment will aid affordability while loosening credit conditions can pump up demand for properties, albeit perhaps less sustainably. Some hard commodities, like steel and copper, are also linked to this housing cycle. With steel being used earlier in the build process than copper, the relative demand movements are also sometimes used as a signal of the development cycle. Both also have widespread commercial applications too, as indeed do other industrial metals like aluminium, nickel and tin. Demand for these will be heavily influenced by the global industrial cycle.

Supply of industrial metals is typically related to mining or smelting capacity. Scheduled maintenance, damage or strikes can cause short-term supply squeezes. However, most metals are bought in advance, so the delivery requirements are reasonably well known by the specialists fulfilling the orders and temporary fluctuations in supply can be smoothed through warehoused capacity. A special class of so-called rare earth metals is not all that rare, but concentrations can create unusually narrow national reliance on them. Their widespread use in modern electronic equipment, including for the defence industry makes it an especially sensitive area. Geopolitical pressures can also be critical for these extremely valuable commodities, even when that pressure is just a politician maximising monopolist profits.

Precious metals, like gold, silver and platinum, also have restrictions on their supply, hence their notorious preciousness. The limited growth of gold supplies was one of the features that made it attractive as a monetary anchor because of that kept inflation at bay. However, gold no longer provides much of a role in the global monetary system. Many central banks still have some gold reserves, but they have fallen to very low shares of the money supply and also of external liabilities. Marginal demand for gold does not come from central banks, although supply sometimes does as these reserves get sold down. The use of precious metals in jewellery and other decorative items remains a major source of demand, especially from India. Financially speaking, though, changes in the demand and prices of precious metals are mainly driven by market risk sentiment. When investors worry about the real outlook, they flock for the safety of gold, bonds and the US dollar. If inflation is also worryingly strong, the real nature of gold means it will become even more attractive as a warehoused store of wealth.

8.3.2 Energy

Some energy commodities, like oil and gas, can also be stored to some degree. However, this task is much harder than with metals. Fuels are dangerously combustible, so safety precautions are needed that inevitably constrains storage capacity. As fluids, containers for oil and gas naturally need to be of a far superior specification to those only holding solids. Building storage capacity is accordingly more expensive and time-consuming amid the necessary permits, such that this space is relatively fixed in the short term. When storage is nearly full, an excess supply of oil and gas can cause relatively large moves in the market. An immediate use for it will need to be found if it can't be stored away and that marginal bid might be very low. In reverse, an excess of demand when storage is running dry could cause a spike in prices as some of that demand will need to be destroyed. Many countries hold strategic energy reserves in the interests of avoiding any extreme squeezes, but by using them, the backstop shrinks and that does not always provide comfort to investors.

Power prices are much more extreme than other energy commodities in their volatility. It is a sort of case study in how others might trade if storage was not an option, even in the short term. Batteries are uneconomically expensive, and other forms of electricity storage are not in widespread use. For example, by pumping water uphill, potential energy is stored that can be utilised upon letting it flow back down through a turbine. Without scope to store an excess supply of electricity, the price can spike unusually high before enough demand is destroyed. Some companies agree subsidies to cease production if the shortfall becomes too large, while some power stations will be paid to have capacity on standby for the same reason. Such arrangements are expensive, but they constrain the size of any imbalance between supply and demand.

The government isn't always overly concerned about creating squeezes in energy-related markets. In particular, most are keen to constrain carbon emissions and the associated negative social externalities. A cap on each company's emissions would do this, but it would pay little regard to the costs of cutting emissions. A fast-growing company could find itself stunted while a vast and inefficient organisation can lumber on, even if it can make reductions at little cost. The solution of sorts has been to create a tradable market in emissions where the highest bidder potentially buys pollution permits. That means those who can reduce emissions at the lowest cost are the ones who should end up doing so. The problem is that some companies can choose to sell any permits they have and shift production to another country outside of the emissions trading scheme, which does not benefit the environment or the country losing activity. Such trades reduce demand and without a supply reduction, will lower the carbon price in the market. The same would be true of technological improvements. Otherwise, demand pressures on prices are procyclically linked to economic activity, and the supply remains a function of regulation.

8.4 Equities

Like holdings of physical commodities, equities don't have a maturity date. However, an equity holding cannot be directly consumed or invested as a productive input, so its value and trading are determined very differently. Equity holders own a share of the company and can expect to earn a portion of its future profitability. Unlike fixed income assets, there is no commitment to pay regular sums to common stockholders, though. Future cash flows nonetheless need to be discounted into assessments of fair value. Two primary valuation models exist for this, with some shortcuts pursued in practice. Particularly from a macroperspective, it is more natural to screen investments based on the sort of factors that should outperform in the anticipated environment. Exploration of such factors will end this section after addressing the valuation models.

8.4.1 Valuation Models

The current price of a share in a company should reflect its proportion of all discounted future cash flows. This theory is the essence of the dividend discount model (DDM). Most companies pay dividends in good times, and some have such well-engrained dividends that investors buy on the condition it stays. Whether the dividend is paid in cash or more shares ("scrip") doesn't matter too much, but it saves broker fees and taxes in some jurisdictions. Other companies prefer to retain earnings instead, but that is only a deferral on when that cash flow can be realised either as future dividends or a share buyback. When dividends are rare or non-existent, it might be more efficient to use discounted free cash flow instead of dividends within the DDM.

For a given expected dividend profile and future price projection, the expected return of a share can be calculated and used for asset allocation purposes. Determining future dividends is difficult, and many analysts make simplifying assumptions, like a constant growth in dividend payments. This simplifies the DDM down to the so-called Gordon model, which can, in turn, be rearranged to say that the expected return is the dividend yield plus that constant growth rate. The results remain highly sensitive to some assumed values, but it is at least easier and more intuitive to calculate when expressed this way. A less sensitive approach to estimating the expected return can be calculated from the incomes retained by the company. This method is the residual income valuation model (RIM), and it involves taking the book value per share and adding the present value of the expected residual income per share. That residual is just the earnings after dividend, which is the clean surplus.

In either case, the discounting of future dividends, free cash flow or retained income, means monetary policy is intricately linked. If a central bank tightens policy and this discount rate rises, the value of future flows will fall in the discounted present. For a given future share price expectation, the expected return will have risen. In an environment, when the economy is doing well enough to justify monetary tightening that fall in current prices may not be undesirable. If the increase is premature or for bad reasons, the outlook for the company could also weaken, thereby causing another downward effect on current prices too. Finally, if tightening is seen on the soft side of what is necessary, the company's outlook will improve, at least in nominal terms, which will raise expectations for the future price. Even the additional discounting of that future state need not cause the current share price to suffer.

When current prices change in response to a differently discounted future, other simple valuation metrics will be revealing different multiples. In particular, the price to earnings (P/E) ratio will have been compressed or expanded by higher or lower rates, respectively. Analysts covering specific companies will often derive their price targets by building models of earnings and multiplying the result by an assumed P/E ratio. That ratio will vary a bit between companies but might be fairly similar across a sector, in which case errors in the assumed multiple matters less when picking sectoral winners and losers to trade. When the earnings yield (inverse of the P/E) or profit per share is low, there are warning signs that the multiple might be overstretched. If profits are failing to cover the dividend, its sustainability must also be questioned even if the dividend yield looks good. Countless ratios can be calculated for some use or another and in a large investment universe, it is important to screen for stories that fit the expected narrative. That leaves a role for factor investing, especially for macroinvestors.

8.4.2 Factor Investing

There are three broad types of factor models that are used by equity investors. Least useful for the economist is statistical factor models. These use methods like principal component analysis to extract common factors that explain the comovement of many asset prices. There is no economic meaning of those statistical artefacts until one can be derived afterwards. Avoiding

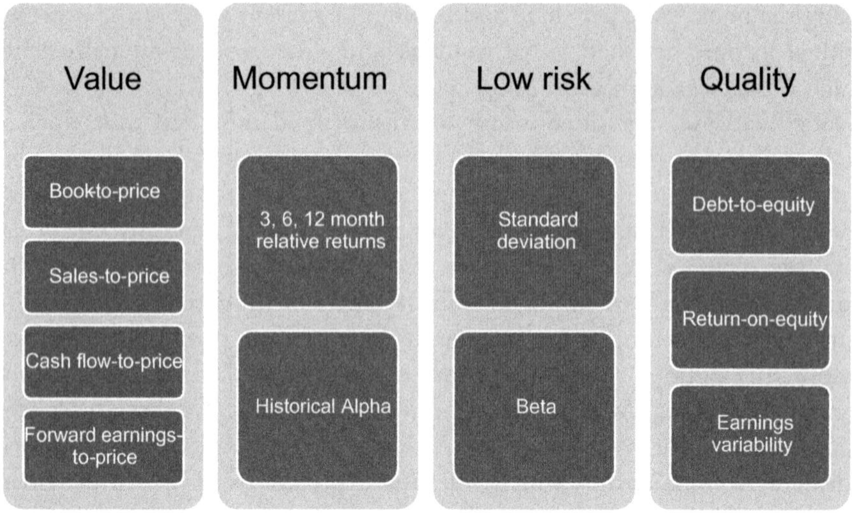

Fig. 8.2 Fundamental factor models

this statistical step are macroeconomic factor models, which instead estimate the sensitivity of shares to various economic factors. Classic examples are investor confidence, inflation, real activity or changes in other markets like the currency. By estimating the market price for that risk factor and the sensitivity of each stock to those risks, expected returns can be built up for each stock that has an economic foundation.

Screening for economic factors is often more of a cross-check of risk exposures than an investment strategy. Fundamental factor models are the third broad type, and they focus more on equity than macroeconomic fundamentals. Some of the most popular are value, momentum, low risk and quality, using some of the metrics listed in Fig. 8.2. The value and momentum factors tend to do well when risk appetite is good, and markets are trending higher, but they also underperform in characteristically steep downturns. Procyclical macroviews are, therefore, more consistent with favouring exposure to these factors, or indeed smaller companies. In contrast, the low-risk factor naturally outperforms in downturns where it pays to be positioned defensively. That similarly means quality companies perform defensively and high yielding ones also tend to do well as investors become drawn to the dividend and what tends to be the relatively stable utility-like businesses that are paying them.

Factors help identify the underlying risks of each share, and investors can use that to consider whether they want to be running that risk in a given macroeconomic environment. A rash of funds has launched since the great recession that turns these factors into investible smart-beta vehicles. By not using market weightings at their core, they help distinguish themselves from some of the problems with conventional asset allocation models. And some of the factors are attractively intuitive. However, many of the factors are unclear, and the selective process can amount to active investing by another name. That is, of course, part of the attraction when it is done properly. Relating the risks back to real macrovariables like growth or monetary policy and the macroviews on those things remains relevant.

8.5 Derivatives

All of the assets discussed so far in this chapter have been relatively straightforward instruments, where there is a direct investment in the underlying security. However, there is a broad class of instruments that derive their value from these more basic underlying instruments. Simplest of them are the forwards and futures that introduce a time dimension to the investment. By some definitions, the exchange of cash flows in the future makes them a basic type of swap. Swaps will often involve cash flows on several dates, though, and mark an exchange over more than just time. These are all linear instruments, though. Options allow highly nonlinear payoff profiles to be created through the buying and selling of contingent rights and responsibilities. The use of all these types of derivatives is widespread among those seeking to speculate on specific views and also those hedging other positions.

8.5.1 Futures

If you're buying an asset now, you need to pay for it now, which requires willingness beyond the desire to take a particular risk. Significant capital needs to back up the position. A bilateral commitment might instead be made to transact at a specific price in the future. As market prices move away from that agreed price, profit or loss will be accrued, despite the transaction of the underlying itself not taking place until the future. When the agreement is reached privately between two parties, this trade is called a forward, and it is a relatively capital efficient way of taking the risk. There is counterparty credit risk involved because it relies on one party having the funds to deliver their side of their agreement. Forwards also contribute to the complex web of linkages between financial institutions, not least because an uncompetitive price to unwind a forward trade encourages an offsetting trade to be placed elsewhere.

Regulators dislike opacity and excessive linkages so they have been encouraging investors to settle trades centrally where they can be seen and net off. Futures are like forwards, but they have standardised terms so they can trade on exchanges. For example, the contract size and delivery terms will be fixed. The underlying asset might be a government bond benchmark, currency, commodity or equity index, but it will be something that market participants care enough about to trade regularly. The existence of a future can also make the related underlying market a better liquidity point. If a market maker buys a 10-year US Treasury without a buyer lined up or the desire to be long that trader can immediately sell 10-year UST futures with an equivalent underlying size. The exposure to changes in the underlying price has been covered in this so-called delta hedge. Alternatively, someone might have a view on strong economic data or a hawkish policy statement and want to take a punt by hitting the future, which can be quickly unwound later, hopefully with some profits locked in.

Standardisation means that there are far more assets without an aligned future than there are with liquid futures trading. A future on a neighbouring bond might be a suitable compromise, where the duration of the futures position can be calibrated to match that of the underlying bond, but the difference means there is an inconsistency. The futures price will not converge to the right underlying, so it is an imperfect hedge, where the gap is known as basis risk. Futures will typically trade with delivery dates in each quarter or month, so there is some room to align hedges. However, the majority of dates might trade very infrequently, and an absence of liquidity will make it harder to transact in size. Traders placing speculative positions will often choose to roll their positions onto the next contract to maintain liquidity in the position and avoid delivery if it is a very short-term future being held.

Sequential contracts don't typically trade at the same price, and there are brokerage fees, so rolling contracts can cost money, depending on the shape of the futures curve. For commodities, the curve needs to take account of expected changes in the balance between supply and demand. For non-perishable products, the costs of storage and the convenience yield of owning them will also influence the curve, because demand is deferrable. The slope should mainly depend on storage and financing costs because these create the costs of carrying positions, while supply imbalances will bleed into the level of the wider curve. Because futures will settle at the spot price, they should converge to expectations of where the spot price will be, especially as delivery nears. The yield during this convergence between the futures price and spot is known as the roll yield. An upward sloping portion of a commodities futures curve is in "contango" while an inverted curve that slopes down is called normal backwardation. Contango curves roll-down to the spot so have negative roll yield while the opposite is true for curves in backwardation. Traditionally, the crude oil curve is humped, but it might be mostly upward or downward sloping at times too.

For equity indices, futures can also be a useful tool for hedging or otherwise altering the sensitivity of the portfolio to the overall market, otherwise known as its beta. If the portfolio has a beta above one but the portfolio manager wants to subtract the systemic market risk, an equivalent multiple of the future can be sold short to take the beta to zero. When there is more confidence in the stock picking than the market outlook, this approach may be advisable. Alternatively, a portfolio's beta might be defensively below one, but fear of underperforming a market benchmark in an extended bullish run would justify temporarily raising that by buying futures. Any portfolio beta can be targeted in this way.

Perhaps the most direct way of implementing broad economic views in markets, though, is to use the interest rate futures that currently settle against interbank rates (LIBOR). These rates are strongly related to the policy rate so bullish views on the economy or hawkish ones on monetary policy should see these rates higher. And vice versa for bearish and dovish views. Rather than taking outright positions on the Short Sterling, or Eurodollar curve for example, the position might be more cleanly and cheaply expressed as a spread. For example, buying M9 Short Sterling and selling M9 Eurodollar is a gloomy UK trade that reduces the potential for US strength to overwhelm the view. Alternatively, different points in the curve can be bought and sold as steepening or flattening trades that also affect the cost of holding the position. Such curve trades can also be expressed relative to another country, where the four legs make it a box trade. Between the different dates, currencies and underlying rates, there is significant flexibility to express all manner of economic views. Indeed, finding the best one is a big part of a rates strategist's job.

8.5.2 Swaps

A series of short-term interest rate futures can be accumulated into a total yield for that period, which would vary with shifts in interest rate expectations. One of the banking system's core functions is maturity transformation, where it borrows short term and lend long term. That means its costs are more likely than its revenues to follow something related to this series of short-term rates. A bank may wish to swap some of those variable rate payments for a fixed rate to reduce its exposure to a hawkish surprise. It can do exactly this with a plain vanilla interest rate swap, where it will pay fixed and receive floating rates. In general terms, a swap is an agreement to exchange cash flows in the future, and there are many sorts, but this is the most common type. It is useful for hedging real liabilities of the short-term type discussed already but is also helpful for pension and insurance funds with long-term liabilities. Speculators often enjoy constructing complex swap trades with many legs, sometimes in forward space, like the 5-yr rate in 5-yr time. Such trades might be targeted at particular market views or just exploiting quirks in the prices being offered by others.

Relative swap trades can be expressed as spreads in multiple currencies where floating rates of one currency are exchanged for fixed rates in another. Currency swaps can also align things differently, though. In their simplest and standard form, two-streams of money market floating rates are exchanged in two currencies. They are commonly called cross-currency swaps and are used to fund foreign currency assets, convert liabilities or to arbitrage. For example, a company might be able to access cheaper funding in one currency than the one it sees the most profitable investment. This swap has the effect of financing the investment in that other currency. Some institutional investors (especially from Japan) are required to hedge their foreign purchases, usually by constantly rolling short-term foreign exchange swaps, so they will consider international investments based on the relative FX-hedged returns.

At the start of the currency swap, one side will agree to pay the other a fixed spread beyond the floating interest rate payments. This spread is essentially the shadow price of borrowing a given currency abroad, and it is called the FX basis. When this basis is very low, the price of US dollar funding offshore has increased, and this might be a sign of financial distress. US dollars are the international reserve currency and are needed for the smooth functioning of the system, so shortages are worrying. However, low periods can also be benignly motivated by pre-funding ahead of potential rate rises. That is a temporary problem of excess demand rather than a shortage of supply. Imbalanced cross-border investment can forewarn asset-driven basis widening, while liability-driven pressures would tend to accompany other signs of stress, like wider spreads between interest rate swaps and bonds. Unlike liability-driven widening, there is a natural limit on asset-driven basis widening as buyers will lose interest in buying an asset with FX hedge in place once the cost of the hedge exceeds the expected return.

As a swap is simply an agreed future exchange of cash flows, there are many types in circulation across various asset classes. Credit portfolios can be insured with credit default swaps (CDS), which pay out when default events are recorded. They got a bad reputation during the euro area sovereign debt crisis when CDS was actively traded in the absence of a liquid underlying bond market, but debt restructurings were carefully arranged to avoid triggers. The use of CDS to synthetically create CDO's also appeared like a step of financial engineering too far for many people. More mundane swaps also exist in conventional markets. Equity swaps exchange the total return of an index (dividends and the capital gains) for either a fixed or floating interest rate. Commodity swaps use a series of forward contracts. There are even weather swaps that exchange a fixed cash flow for a floating leg derived from the sum of heating degree days. Swaps are only limited by the imagination of financial engineers and the willingness of fund managers and company treasurers to trade exotic structures. If there is a particular complex view you want to express and you have the funds to risk, there will be a queue of people willing to structure it for you, at a price of course.

8.5.3 Options

Futures and swaps have a linear relationship with their underlying, but that doesn't have to be the case. Derivatives can be constructed to yield all manner of complex payoff profiles. The basic building blocks of these trades are call and put options. Buying the former confers the right, but not the obligation, to buy a given security at a specified price. The put is the same but about the right to sell the security. Buying either carries a maximum loss of the initial premium being paid, while the potential profit is unlimited. Selling either yields the opposite, with a small premium being picked up as compensation for adopting unlimited potential losses (Fig. 8.3).

When an option's strike price is at a level where it would not trigger, it is classed as out of the money. The further an option is out of the money, the cheaper it will be. Higher volatility environments will raise an option's premium because it becomes more likely that the option will expire with the underlying asset trading at a price where it profitably triggers. As time passes and the option expiry nears, any given level of volatility would struggle to take it as far into the money, so time naturally decays an option's premium. By combining calls and puts, more complex payoff profiles can be constructed, some of which amount to trades on volatility itself. Straddles can do so while offering unlimited upside. Butterflies curtail the gains and reduce the cost, while condors cheapen further amid a reduced likelihood of expiring in the money (Fig. 8.4).

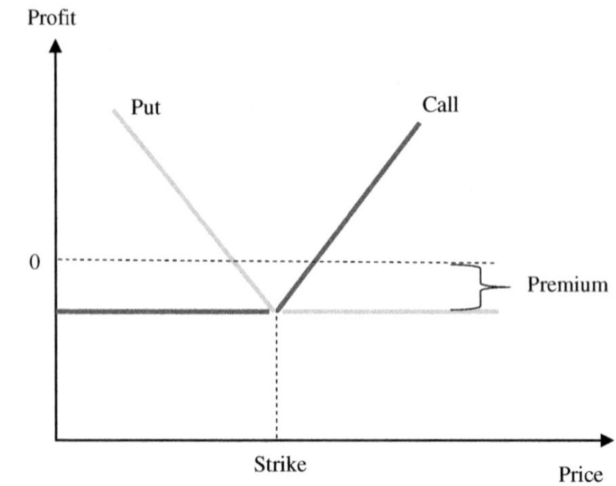

Fig. 8.3 Call and put payoff profiles

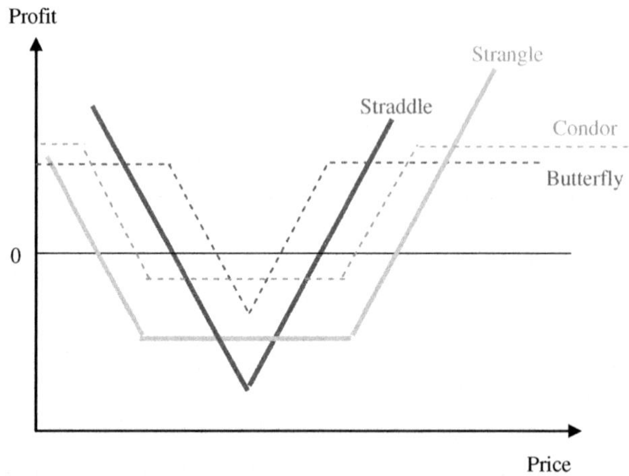

Fig. 8.4 Volatility strategy payoff profiles

Many traders, especially in hedge funds, like to sell volatility. In doing so, they collect small but regular premiums that look like wonderfully stable and uncorrelated returns to their investors. However, if the strategy is pursued too long, the profitable patch can end in a spectacular blow up or at least a sizeable draw down. It is a bit like picking up pennies in front of a steamroller in the sense you might get flattened for doing it. Slightly more sustainable is to use options to position around potential breakout occasions. Some of those might be related to a macroevent, although such positions can become expensively crowded. Setting strikes around key technical levels is another approach to take for those keen to get in early. Buying options can be an attractive way to hedge tail risks in a portfolio. If the risk doesn't crystallise, not much is lost, but if it does, profits on an option book can make all the difference. Before the tail risk can be hedged, though, a portfolio must first be optimally constructed. How to do that is the focus of the next chapter.

Main Messages

- Correlation can be confused for causality in egregious data mining exercises spuriously back fitting recent price moves. However, when enough of the market is looking at the same levels to buy or sell at, technical factors can nonetheless be self-fulfilling.
- Many of the best macrotraders will time when they enter their fundamental positions by referring to simple technical factors like turning points around recent trends, reversal proportions of previous moves or moving averages of price action.
- When the expected cash requirement changes during the year, it is sometimes advisable for a government to amend the stock of Bill issuance rather than change bond issuance programmes or fiscal policy.
- Monetary policy tends to provide the anchor for the discount rate, sometimes explicitly when the central bank is itself issuing Bills to sterilise the stock of reserves. Supply of Bills relative to the demand for them in repos or as safe liquid assets will then determine the tradeable price around that policy anchor.
- Bonds with high coupons will be paying out more of their value at earlier periods, so the traded price will be less sensitive to changes in yield than one with low coupons and back-loaded income. This effect is measured by a bond's duration, which is intuitively the average time to receive all the cash flows.
- Duration is technically a first-order approximation that will underestimate the price change associated with a given yield change. Bond convexity adjusts for this error, and it is a positive function of cash-flow dispersion and duration.
- Interest rate levels will move in response to changes in either the expected path for monetary policy or term premium. Term premium is the additional compensation investors demand for holding long duration assets.

Concerns about the credit quality of the issuer or the liquidity of the security can affect it.

- Pools of debt can be combined to provide the investor with diversification across a range of issues. The resultant repackaged (securitised) bonds should, therefore, be less susceptible to idiosyncratic shocks, which reduces the risk profile and risk-adjusted returns by extension.
- Expressing and analysing opinions relative to a basket of currencies can help sterilise the potential for surprise in one to overwhelm an economic view on another.
- Uncovered interest parity (UIP) and purchasing power parity (PPP) are the two arbitrage conditions in foreign exchange. PPP provides a theoretical anchor for the level and UIP for the adjustment path. Neither is a powerful predictor of currency moves.
- Many market participants trade the explicit view that UIP doesn't hold. By buying a high yielding currency with a low-yielding one, the investor can potentially receive a favourable yield differential. This practice is called a carry trade.
- Probably the most popular exchange rate model is for the behavioural equilibrium exchange rate (BEER). The primary variables involve the terms of trade, net foreign assets, relative fiscal policy and productivity.
- Underlying balance models treat the real exchange rate as a relative price that must move to bring supply and demand to equilibrium. The fundamental equilibrium exchange rate (FEER) is not the equilibrium level at all times, though, since it also relies upon internal balance being achieved.
- Financial fair value (FFV) models estimate the historical relationship between changes in FX and the price of other asset classes.
- Commodities are real assets with an intrinsic use for consumption or investment. This distinctive quality means that commodities can provide some diversification benefits to a portfolio and increase risk-adjusted returns.
- When storage is nearly full, an excess supply of commodities can cause relatively large moves in the market. The opposite is also true when storage is running dry, and demand must be destroyed.
- The current price of a share in a company should reflect its proportion of all discounted future cash flows. This theory is the essence of the dividend discount model (DDM).
- The residual income valuation model (RIM) takes the book value per share and adds the present value of the expected residual income per share. That residual is just the earnings after dividend, which is the clean surplus.

- If a central bank tightens policy and this discount rate rises, the value of future flows will fall in the discounted present.
- Screening for economic factors is often more of a cross-check of risk exposures than an investment strategy.
- Fundamental factors help identify the underlying risks of each share and investors can use that to consider whether they want to be running that risk in a given macroeconomic environment.
- Derivatives derive their value from more basic underlying instruments. Simplest of them are the forwards and futures that introduce a time dimension to the investment. Futures are like forwards, but they have standardised terms so they can trade on exchanges.
- An upward sloping portion of a commodities futures curve is in "contango" while an inverted curve that slopes down is called normal backwardation. Contango curves roll down to the spot so have negative roll yield while the opposite is true for curves in backwardation.
- If an equity portfolio has a beta above one but the portfolio manager wants to subtract the systemic market risk, an equivalent multiple of the index future can be sold short to take the beta to zero.
- Perhaps the most direct way of implementing broad economic views in markets, though, is to use the interest rate futures that currently settle against interbank rates. A position might be more cleanly and cheaply expressed as a spread or different points in the curve can be bought and sold as steepening or flattening trades.
- Cross-currency swaps are used to fund foreign currency assets, convert liabilities and to arbitrage. They have the effect of financing investment in another currency.
- The shadow price of borrowing a given currency abroad is called the FX basis. It can widen because of pressures from assets or liabilities. Unlike liability-driven widening, there is a natural limit on asset-driven basis widening as buyers will lose interest in buying an asset with an FX hedge in place once the cost of the hedge exceeds the expected return.
- Futures and swaps have a linear relationship with their underlying, but that doesn't have to be the case. Derivatives can be constructed to yield all manner of complex payoff profiles. The basic building blocks of these trades are call and put options.
- Some option strategies amount to trades on volatility. Straddles do so while offering unlimited upside. Butterflies curtail the gains and reduce the cost, while condors cheapen further amid a reduced likelihood of expiring in the money.

- Selling volatility is a bit like picking up pennies in front of a steamroller in the sense you make a small return, but might get flattened for doing it.
- Buying options can be an attractive way to hedge tail risks in a portfolio. If the risk doesn't crystallise, not much is lost, but if it does, profits on an option book can make all the difference.

Further Reading

Driver, Rebecca. Westaway, Peter. 2004. *Concepts of equilibrium exchange rates*. Working Paper No. 248. Bank of England.

Hull, John. 2005. *Options, Futures, and Other Derivatives*. Pearson Education.

Fabozzi, Frank. 2005. *Financial Modeling of the Equity Market: From CAPM to Cointegration*. John Wiley & Sons.

Choudhry, Moorad. 2014. *Fixed Income Markets: Management, Trading and Hedging*. John Wiley & Sons.

9
Portfolios

The previous chapter explored the drivers of different asset classes, which portfolio managers will take views on and invest accordingly. Sometimes there won't be many differential views around, and a concentration of positions will accumulate that steadily drives up an asset price. Should that view prove wrong, the run for the exit is much less elegant when in a crowd. Leverage unwinds and a gradual increase in money can be much more rapidly destroyed, causing a sharp correction in the process. Price action can accordingly be described as walking up the stairs and falling down the lift shaft. Recovering after such a fall can be difficult, not least because if a portfolio falls 50% and then rises 50%, it is still down by 25%. Investors might also be demanding their money back, or at least fee concessions if the manager has merely fallen into the same trap as everyone else.

What investors want to see are positive returns that lack variability, skew to the upside and don't have extreme changes. In other terms, they love the odd statistical moments (return and skew) but hate even ones (variance and kurtosis). Delivering consistently favourable returns requires not just getting your main views right, but making sure losses are relatively limited. Doing this encourages the use of mathematical models to combine views and control risk. Sometimes the latter will be left to a risk manager to control, but it is a general responsibility. When targeted investments are heavily correlated, the real risk attached to a view might be unintentionally large, even if prevailing investment risk limits permit the position. Models need not merely provide a cross check on exposures, though, as they can also be used to

P. Rush, *Real Market Economics*,
https://doi.org/10.1057/978-1-349-95278-6_9

drive the investment decisions. The combination of views into constructed portfolios will be addressed later in this chapter, but the main assumptions underlying portfolio theory need consideration first.

9.1 Principles

Portfolio theory answers the economic question of how to optimally allocate resources amid the different expected risks and returns. An economist might view the answer as the intersection of demanded and supplied expected returns relative to the risk of obtaining them. Stated more formally, the demand curve for returns is the expected utility function. This terminological formulation increases the transparency of the problem at hand, whereby investors demand maximum utility (broadly returns as an approximation to wealth) subject to constraints. Meanwhile, the expected supplied returns derive from the joint distribution of all feasible portfolios. Optimal expected supply outcomes form a risk-return curve that is conventionally referred to as the efficient frontier. The issues surrounding these functions are expanded upon below to provide an understanding of the theory underlying the more complex modifications made afterwards.

9.1.1 Demand and Supply

Some behavioural assumptions are made in deriving the expected utility function. Investors are assumed to derive utility from returns and discount utility from the risk associated with those returns, thus creating an upward sloping expected utility indifference schedule. This analysis can be augmented further with a stronger risk aversion assumption where investors demand increasing rates of return for receiving additional risk. As a result, the investors' expected utility function is convex (i.e., the first and second differential of the utility function are both positive). Combinations of expected return and risk can be plotted to form indifference curves with these properties. Investors are assumed to be indifferent between any expected outcome on a given indifference curve because they are perfectly compensated through higher expected returns for assuming increasing levels of risk. Rational investors prefer more utility to less, so a higher expected utility indifference curve is preferable to a lower curve. Formally, in Fig. 9.1, "U2" stochastically dominates "U1".

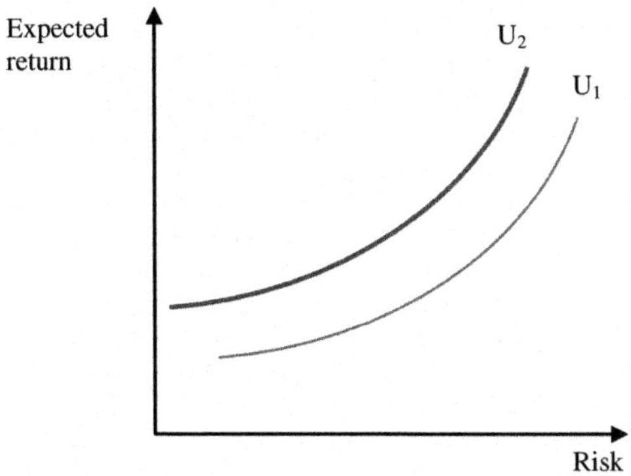

Fig. 9.1 Utility curves

Understanding that investors demand additional returns as compensation for higher risk is an essential theoretical building block. As markets are typically assumed to be efficient, assets that are inherently riskier are usually expected to ultimately yield higher returns as fair compensation to the investors taking those risks. In the capital asset pricing model (CAPM), this amounts to an asset having a higher expected return when its price has historically moved by than one-for-one with the overall market's returns (i.e., its "Beta"). The assumptions needed to make this hold are far removed from reality, but it's a model that can fill in a baseline for investors to tilt away from with forecasts derived from their wider view of the world as it actually is at that time. Alternative approaches are legion and include the simple extrapolation of past returns into the future, despite the notorious warning of past performance being no guarantee of future performance.

More complicated alternatives neither place as much reliance on past returns being reflective of the future or on the assumption that investors are only compensated for the elasticity of an asset's returns to the overall market's movements. Arbitrage Pricing Theory (APT) broadens out the range of systematic risks to any number of plausible factors under the assumption that there is a linear relationship between them and the expected returns. Estimating such a model will often yield insignificant factors to be discarded while the rest are relied upon to remain relevant characteristics of future performance. By using ordinary linear regression techniques to do this, a linear relationship is assumed to exist between these factors and the expected return. APT is, therefore, a generalised version of the CAPM, which some investors might prefer to use as their baseline within asset allocation models.

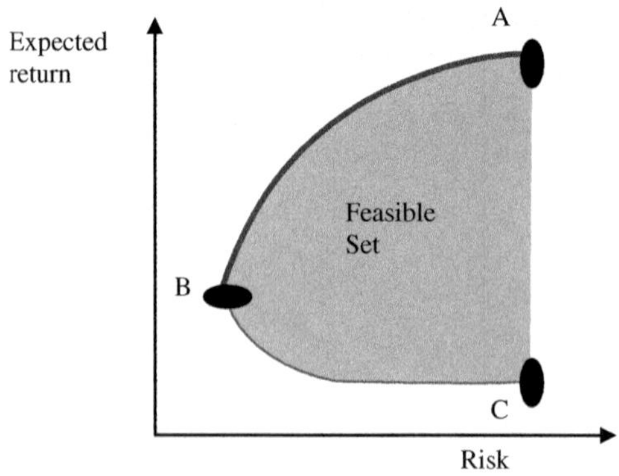

Fig. 9.2 The feasible set

Expectations for the distribution of each asset's returns can be combined to form a set of all possible expected outcomes that can be supplied by the market. Probability theory treats this under joint distributions, the mean of which forms the feasible set in the current portfolio theory context. From among those portfolios which bound the feasible set, those along the line "A–B" in Fig. 9.2 form the efficient frontier. Any portfolio not on the efficient frontier is sub-optimal because investor utility can be increased by either selecting a portfolio with a higher expected return for the same level of risk, or less risk for the same level of return. Line "B–C" can be considered as the inefficient frontier because it forms the lower boundary where the lowest return for any given level of risk is found. Of additional interest is "Point B", which is the global minimum variance portfolio or the global minimal risk portfolio in this case. In the absence of a binding expected return target, this point should be reached, but here it is assumed that investors demand a minimal return.

9.1.2 Diversification

The concept of diversification is one that has been implicitly used in the creation of portfolios such as those comprising the feasible set above. However, diversification's benefits are so fundamental to portfolio theory that a more rigorous justification is required here. If all assets in a portfolio are perfectly correlated (i.e., a correlation of 1), this portfolio will act as though it is comprised of just one asset and so the portfolio's rate of return and variance will equal that asset's return and variance. In this case, there is no benefit of diversification, but it is an unrealistic example. For a second portfolio, assume that the returns on all constituent assets are independent of each other, have a finite variance and are held with an equal weighting. On average, the portfolio's return will be equal to the weighted return of that individual asset. This outcome is a negative feature when considering positive returns, but it is a definite benefit when there are declining asset values. The real benefit from diversification lies in the reduction in portfolio variance from the addition of independently distributed assets to the portfolio. Theoretically, as the number of such assets in the portfolio increases, the portfolio variance should trend towards zero.

In reality, many non-vanishing correlations result in an empirical bound to diversification's benefits. It is only the idiosyncratic risks that can be diversified away to zero, not systemic risks. Because dispersion is an adverse moment to investors, its reduction is beneficial and will cause investors to derive higher utility from the portfolio. The cost of diversification is the loss of extreme upside events, but this is paid for through the reduction in significant downside events and the corresponding decline in variance. The major implication of this is that portfolios comprised of assets with lower absolute correlations should experience less variation. Attention should, therefore, be paid to the correlation of assets when constructing a minimum risk portfolio.

9.2 Portfolio Construction

Most portfolio managers don't attempt to formally optimise where they are investing in the feasible set of potential portfolios. Many will have a benchmark portfolio where their views are aiming to add value relative to that, where the market return is known as beta and the uplift is alpha. Differential views on the economy, policy response or on how the market might perceive those things can lead to outright positions on individual assets, relative ones or favouring of a broader class of assets. This group might be similar securities in a sector or those that thrive under similar circumstances, including when certain styles of factor investing might thrive. Simple rules like momentum are also popular influences. But all of these are influences on the expected return of assets. Optimising the portfolio to take into account the risks within and shared between positions is an art unto itself.

There is a science to the optimisation of portfolios, which is sometimes sold as a black-box strategy. Others are instinctively dismissive about such approaches because there are lots of dodgy assumptions in this field. However, there is a difference between explicitly deferring to a simple model in all areas and using it as a framework for rationalising views that are going to be traded anyway, with other unknown assumptions implicitly made in the process. Several trades might seem great in their own right, but if they amount to different expressions of the same thing, or are highly correlated with something else, it might be desirable to dial down the exposure to them. An optimisation process can help reveal where this is the case and indicate what the best mix of expressions are for that view. And by constraining the concentration and level of risk taken, it is easier for performance to be consistent and replicable, not that either can ever be guaranteed in the real world of course.

9.2.1 Mean-Variance

One of the earliest, easiest and most popular forms of controlling the level of risk in a portfolio was created by Markowitz and is sometimes referred to by his name. In his approach, a given level of returns is targeted and the expected variance of the portfolio minimised by optimising to that point in the efficient set. Variance is a bad risk measure because it penalises upside and downside shocks to returns equally, despite the upside being actively sought. Nonetheless, investor utility is better approximated by including this, the second statistical moment, and thus assuming quadratic utility and normally distributed returns, instead of risk indifference. It is around here that portfolio management must move beyond simple spreadsheets as quadratic optimisation functions need to be solved. Efficient algorithms exist for this and can be programmed to search for the local optimal solution.

In essence, the objective function is to minimise the variance of the portfolio subject to the constraint of expecting to exceed a predefined level of return. A baseline for the expected returns might be derived empirically under the ambitious assumption that returns will be equal to recent experience or be informed by other views or models like the CAPM. Meanwhile, the targeted returns are a function of the feasible range of expected returns and the risk aversion of the investor. The covariance matrix measures risk, which tends to be taken from a recently observed sample. That is arguably a less unrealistic assumption, although the tendency for correlations to spike in a stressed scenario is something that needs consideration. If such a situation is anticipated in the portfolio's construction, it might be better to draw the covariance matrix from a similar historical episode.

Of the other constraints applied to the optimizer, the lower bound is often set at zero to prevent short selling, although that is not necessarily a binding problem for all portfolios. And on the other side, an upper bound is usually set to ensure a minimum number of assets (e.g. 0.5 for two assets) are constructing a diversified portfolio. Without the ceiling and with some short selling allowed, the optimizer could plausibly find positions where it seeks high allocations to particular assets as it leverages up the portfolio. Finally, an equality condition is needed to define a budget constraint, which forces the sum of all weights to be less than or equal to one. Unlike a bank, the investor can't create money to fund purchases beyond the resources it already has, other than to the extent the newly bought assets are used to raise finance afterwards.

Although this mean-variance approach is a significant improvement over simple rules that are ignorant to risk, it remains ignorant in ways that make it an inadequate risk measure. Penalising positive and negative variance equally and assuming that returns are normally distributed are not realistic. Returns are typically negatively skewed (not symmetric as under a normal distribution) and exhibit fatter tails (kurtosis not equal to three). Violation of the normal distribution assumption means other methods are required to focus on the lower tail of the distribution of returns. Frequently, this causes risk managers to focus on the Value at Risk (VaR) in a portfolio. Portfolio managers are drilled into following this, both for their use and the effect that it has on wider market dynamics. It is a concept that can also be beneficially applied in other approaches to quantitative portfolio management where positions are formally optimised without as many of the dodgy assumptions.

9.2.2 Value at Risk (VaR)

Acknowledging that it is financial losses that investors are averse to means other measures of risk naturally need to be sought, besides variance. Focusing on the tail of the returns distribution is Value at Risk (VaR), which attempts to quantify the loss (α) that is expected to occur with a specified probability (β). Meanwhile, Conditional Value at Risk (CVaR) is the mean expected loss beyond the value at risk (α), and it contains more information about the adverse tail (Fig. 9.3). It is arguably a better measure of risk as a result, and it is also easier to optimise.

One problem with VaR is that it isn't additive in the sense that a combination of two portfolios could be deemed to have greater than the sum of the risks. The benefits of diversification are not calculated. Furthermore, unlike CVaR, there is no accounting for the size of the losses beyond the value at risk. Minimisation of a portfolio's VaR can thus lead to the tail exceeding VaR to be stretched out, leading to higher average losses during negative scenarios. Unfortunately, VaR is only a coherent risk measure

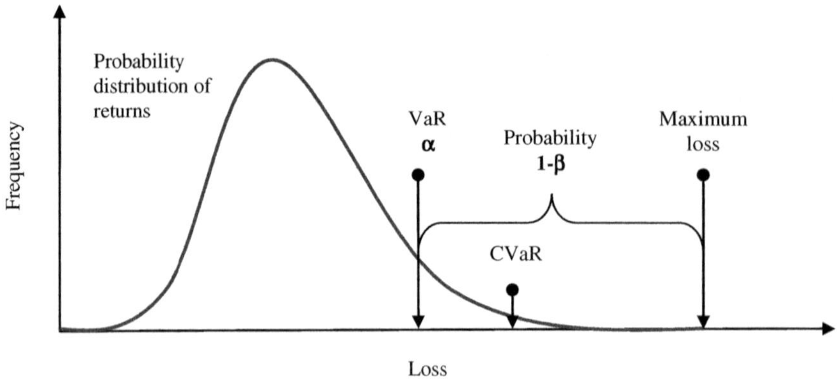

Fig. 9.3 Conditional value at risk

when it is based upon normally distributed returns, which is a rare phenomenon in the financial world. If VaR is relied upon excessively, an investor might inadvertently be running more risk than expected. Or a less scrupulous trader might choose to allocate risk in areas where VaR is an especially poor indicator. For example, options have nonlinear return distributions by design, so selling out of the money ones picks up a little premium without much variance in the current value under normal circumstances, but as the option nears the strike price, losses balloon. VaR does not capture this and nor would it do so with other assets where stressed scenarios have not occurred during its trading history. Such shortfalls make its dominance as the risk measure for regulators all the more concerning.

There is no magic solution to the issue of approximating the true distribution of returns as only a sample is ever observable. Bigger samples should be more representative of the real distribution and so longer sample periods make it more likely that similar scenarios will have occurred before. Where short histories exist, creating a proxy for old behaviours could be worthwhile, especially if the asset has never traded through stressed scenarios before. Similar securities or derivatives may have done and will probably be a better guide than to ignore such events entirely. This process might be expedited by using parametric methods to fit a plausible distribution that includes unobserved adverse scenarios. When the beginning of a negative shock is seen after a period of calm, VaR models might otherwise abruptly incorporate the downside risk, causing many investors to reduce the risk to stay within permitted levels. That is a "VaR shock", and they can sometimes be anticipated.

Whether the distribution's parameters are empirically estimated from its history or imposed, the joint probability distribution needs to be assembled in order to calculate the CVaR. It lends itself to optimisation far better than VaR, which is a non-smooth, non-convex and multi-extremal function with respect to positions. In other words, the optimal solution depends on the starting weights and need not lead to the actual optimum at all. In comparison, CVaR optimisation can be defined as a relatively straightforward linear problem. The linear programming methods needing to solve such optimisation problems are efficient even for vast portfolios, and the subroutines for this are fairly widely available.

During the optimisation process, a starting vector will be provided based upon the weights and VaR for the baseline portfolio, which might be something like an equally weighted portfolio. This vector is then adjusted within the optimizer until reaching the minimum. As with the mean-variance approach, some constraints feed into the optimizer. In essence, the first restriction constitutes a requirement to meet a minimum level of returns. The second is typically a budget constraint, while the third is both a ban on short selling and leverage. In addition to minimising CVaR, the portfolio VaR should also be reduced using the optimal weights. Furthermore, each variation in the weights vector constructs new portfolios via stochastic programming, so an attractive empirical dependence structure is used to model coupled risks.

Portfolio performance will naturally depend on the investment universe, period, constraints and assumptions, but in general, optimised portfolios tend to deliver more stable performance. That doesn't mean they are always right. On the contrary, their risk aversion can mean missing out on long periods of bullish performance elsewhere, and that underperformance can be difficult for portfolio managers to explain away. Moreover, CVaR-minimised portfolios can be more prone to buying into frothy markets than equivalents using a mean-variance strategy. This weakness is because no penalty is applied unless the asset exhibits an expensive lower tail, which is not always the case with assets on an unrelenting upward trajectory, even if it is ultimately unsustainable. In either approach, there is a role for applying a judgmental overlay. Sometimes that overlay will subtract from the model's strength, but by providing informational context outside of the standard black box, enhanced performance is possible. Such models are perhaps best used as part of an overall asset allocation framework where they can impart discipline and aid consistency.

9.2.3 Utility Maximisation

In both the mean-variance and CVaR optimisations introduced above, the objective was to target a given level of return and minimise risk subject to the expectation of achieving that. This ordering might seem a little odd, though. Many investors have some tolerance for risk and instead want to maximise returns subject to not exceeding that risk level. Plausible utility functions have occasionally been imposed to fit alongside stylised return distributions. This approach would frequently assume quadratic utility and normal return distributions, but both remain a rough approximation and will not suit all investors. Incorporating higher moments typically violates these assumptions and mandates further investigation.

Parameterisation of higher statistical moments within the utility maximisation space is directionally intuitive (investor preferences for positive returns and skewness but an aversion to dispersion and kurtosis are well known) but quantifying parameters is tricky. Haim Levy first proposed higher moment utility approximation as a Taylor Series expansion in 1969. However, optimisation of these approximated utility functions is computationally intensive and has only recently come within the scope of computing. The attractive resultant modelling of coskewness and cokurtosis becomes analytically complicated because calculations occur using rank-3 and rank-4 tensors. To see why, just try visualising beyond vectors and matrices to plot the additional dimensions as cubes and hypercubes, respectively. A lot of mental dexterity is needed to conceive the problems, let alone cumbersomely solve them.

Detailing a thorough approach to optimising utility functions is beyond the scope of this book, but for those seeking a guideline, it involves initially deriving preference parameters for each statistical moment. A Markov Chain Monte Carlo estimation routine can then be used to draw predictive summaries and estimate the approximate expected utility as an ergodic average. Numerical optimisation can then occur using the Metropolis-Hastings (MH) algorithm to explore the projected utility function with the most frequently visited weights maximising utility. MH is known to be effective in the searching of high dimensional spaces, and moreover, the MH algorithm will find the global maximum

9.2.4 Combining Views

Optimisers alone can provide considerable assistance in a quantitative investment process, but the ones discussed so far are unlikely to be sufficient for most portfolio managers. Some investors will want a quantitative framework that is better able to reflect the real world within the black box. Others will want to feed in their insights flexibly. Probably the most widely used asset allocation model for the latter is the Black-Litterman one. It was originally published in 1990, and it relies on some well-known unrealistic assumptions, but it is far from alone in using them. In particular, the baseline expectations for asset price returns usually derive from the Capital Asset Pricing Model, which assumes that markets are efficient and returns are normally distributed. The CAPM provides a justification, albeit flawed, for using the market capitalisation weighted portfolio as the starting benchmark in the model. From that point, mean-variance optimisation derives efficient deviations towards a more desirable portfolio.

The added value of the Black-Litterman model is in the way it allows the user to tilt towards views that the investor wants to incorporate. If the expected returns are merely overwritten by the investor's opinion in a standard optimizer, the impact on weightings can sometimes seem surprising and at odds with where the genuine conviction exists. That is because the change in expected returns will shift the feasible set of expected returns and risk such that different combinations will now deliver the efficient frontier. A view that US equities might outperform Canadian equities might drive bigger changes in the allocation among European equities, where a conviction view might not exist at all.

When an investor has an opinion on relative performance, the effect on the portfolio's weightings should be concentrated in that area. The Black-Litterman model does this by combining the baseline portfolio with portfolios reflecting the investor's particular views. Many views can feed into the model, and the relative weightings of all the portfolios will depend on confidence levels and the view's distinctiveness. As confidence in an opinion rises or falls, perhaps as more evidence about it accumulates, the weight assigned to that view will also rise and fall. If a view is already reflected in the relative returns of the combined portfolio, it will not have any effect on the asset allocation. Covariance between a view and either other views or the baseline portfolio will also constrain the weight assigned to that opinion in the overall portfolio. Where views on returns are absolute, the investor should be aware that the view is weighted relative to the equilibrium expected returns, rather than the recent performance. A view that an asset's returns will weaken might still be a bullish message for the model that causes an increased allocation towards it if care isn't taken.

Uncertain views are assumed to have a normal distribution around them, as is the case with the underlying asset returns. It is possible to relax just the latter assumption by using so-called Copula-opinion pooling (COP), but that is only a partial fix. For investors seeking to express nonlinear views, perhaps on the lower tail of the distribution or its codependence, a more complex solution is needed. The entropy pooling approach allows this and is also of practical use for funds run by multiple portfolio managers as each can express their own views with different confidence levels and leave the model to reconcile an appropriate average of them all.

The math naturally gets more complicated with incremental improvements to the realism and functionality of asset allocation models. It is a tiny group of people who will ever be involved in the development of such things, though. Code for these models is typically made publicly available, thereby allowing people to utilise them without the need for time-consuming recreation. Analysis of performance is far easier to do in back tests so other users can see the side effects of simplifications even if they can't push the theoretical frontier to fix them. For the vast majority of people using these models, it is only the outputs they will see and then the limitations must just be kept in mind. A model will be wide of the mark when normal distributions are assumed in environments when nonlinear moves are likely, perhaps because of a nonlinear economic shock or inherently nonlinear options in the portfolio.

Main Messages

- Investors want positive returns that lack variability, skew to the upside and don't have extreme changes. In other terms, they love the odd statistical moments (return and skew) but hate the even ones (variance and kurtosis).
- Assets that are inherently riskier are usually expected to ultimately yield higher returns as fair compensation to the investors taking those risks.
- The Capital Asset Pricing Model (CAPM) and Arbitrage Pricing Theory (APT) both use simple linear regressions to estimate the risk factors for an asset relative to the overall market, but CAPM is limited to the beta of returns relative to the market.
- As the number of assets in the portfolio increases, the portfolio variance should reduce. Idiosyncratic risks can be diversified away, but systemic risks cannot because there are many non-vanishing correlations.
- Portfolios comprised of assets with lower absolute correlations should experience less variance. Attention should, therefore, be paid to the correlation of assets when constructing a minimum risk portfolio.
- Most portfolio managers don't formally optimise where they are investing in the feasible set of potential portfolios. Many will have a benchmark portfolio where their views are aiming to add value ("alpha") relative to that.

- The most popular approach to optimising a portfolio is to set an objective function for minimising the variance of the portfolio subject to the constraint of expecting to exceed a predefined level of return.
- Value at Risk (VaR) attempts to quantify the loss (α) that is supposed to occur with a specified probability (β). Meanwhile, Conditional Value at Risk (CVaR) is the mean expected loss beyond the value at risk (α), so it contains more information about the adverse tail.
- Options have nonlinear return distributions by design, so selling out of the money ones picks up a little premium without much variance in the current value under normal circumstances, but as the option nears the strike price, losses can balloon. VaR does not capture this risk.
- Shocks after a period of calm can cause VaR models to abruptly incorporate additional downside risks, thereby causing many investors to reduce risk to stay within permitted levels. That is a "VaR shock", which can sometimes be anticipated among others and sidestepped by assuming a more realistic distribution of returns in the model.
- CVaR lends itself to optimisation far better than VaR, which is a non-smooth, non-convex and multi-extremal function with respect to positions. In other words, the optimal solution depends on the starting weights and need not lead to the actual optimum at all.
- Portfolio performance will naturally depend on the investment universe, period, constraints and assumptions, but in general, optimised portfolios tend to deliver more stable performance.
- Instead of minimising risk, the investor's utility might be maximised instead. However, optimisation of approximated utility functions is computationally intensive and has only recently come within the scope of computing.
- The Black-Litterman model adds value by allowing the user to tilt towards views that the investor wants to incorporate. It then minimises variance subject to a returns target given the model's augmented baseline expectations.
- Covariance between one view and either others or the baseline portfolio will constrain the weight assigned to that opinion in the overall portfolio. Conviction levels will also influence the relative weighting of view portfolios and the baseline.
- For investors seeking to express nonlinear views, perhaps on the lower tail of the distribution or its codependence, a more complex solution like entropy pooling is needed.
- Less sophisticated models will be wide of the mark when normal distributions are assumed in environments when nonlinear moves are likely, perhaps because of a nonlinear economic shock or when inherently nonlinear options are in the portfolio.

Further Reading

Fabozzi, Frank. Kolm, Petter. Pachamanova, Dessislava. Focardi, Sergio. 2007. *Robust Portfolio Optimization and Management.* John Wiley & Sons.

Uryasev, Stanislav. 2000. *Conditional value-at-risk: Optimization algorithms and applications.* Financial Engineering News, 14. February, 1–5.

He, Guangliang. Litterman, Robert. 2002. *The Intuition Behind Black-Litterman Model Portfolios.*

Meucci, Attilio. 2008. *Fully Flexible Views: Theory and Practice.* Risk. 21 (10), 97–102.

10
Epilogue: Future Directions

The first three parts of this book have built a fundamental framework up from basic economic foundations, incorporating the stabilising cross-beams from policymakers before liberally coating it in financial markets. Much of it originated from fairly mainstream theories, but with some augmentations to deal with the quirks of real markets. There are, of course, many economists grappling with the lessons of the Great Recession, which was an episode that highlighted to the world how far economics is from being a perfect science. Some of the resultant research is pushing the theoretical frontiers in exciting new directions, but the majority might acknowledge only a few of the weaker failings. With an incorrect diagnosis, their solutions end up akin to putting lipstick on a pig, to put it politely.

This final chapter emphasises where some of the main flaws are in both theory and focus, to help draw attention to some of the most exciting areas. There is a long way to go before the models can correct for what is intuitively known to be wrong, at least by the non-indoctrinated. And by the very nature of economic dynamics deriving from human actions, perfection will never exist. However, awareness of the problems and conscious attempts to adjust for the past's misfocus can provide an edge over others. In particular, appreciating that real markets are far less linear than conventionally assumed can allow the savvy economist to discount some shocks and emphasise others where a mistaken linearity is opening up significant exploitable gaps. Regulatory change has moved far quicker than the academic adjustments, though. Indeed, those kinds of risk positions will typically trade from

P. Rush, *Real Market Economics*,
https://doi.org/10.1057/978-1-349-95278-6_10

different parts of the financial ecosystem nowadays. Rigorous economic analysis of real markets is still needed from these parts, but that leaves a smaller group of us to operate differently.

10.1 Fixing Fundamental Flaws

In the lead-up to the Great Recession, many economists became emboldened by what former Bank of England Governor Mervyn King calls "the NICE decade"—i.e. the non-inflationary consistently expansionary period. Some believed in the profession's over-hyped omnipotence to the extent that they declared the end of boom and bust economic cycles. Omniscient policymakers would see shocks coming and be able to stimulate away the problems with their powerful tools, or so the hope went. It didn't matter if everyone was drunk on the spiked punch bowl because policymakers could mop up the mess later. But too many economists had drunk too much of their own special Kool-Aid to realise how nonsensical this was. A toxic mixture of bad models and misfocused efforts contributed to the credit crunch, the ensuing Great Recession and the widespread ridicule of economists for failing to see "it" coming. In fairness, some did forecast it, but many were permabears and dismissed accordingly as bitter and bias. It can be awfully tempting to ignore such party poopers when you're having fun.

10.1.1 Bad Models

Perhaps the most worrying aspect of the response to the Great Recession is that the economics profession hasn't fundamentally changed its approach. The same sort of models are still in widespread use, and they are incapable of forecasting the kind of recessionary dynamics that exist in a real economy. If a recession occurred tomorrow, economists would be facing many of the same criticisms again and look all the more foolish for it.

The workhorse macromodel in widespread use remains of the dynamic stochastic general equilibrium (DSGE) variety. These models have a mathematical elegance that yields consistent and smooth simulations and crucially, a hoard of indoctrinated users who build their careers around them. Theoretical shortcomings are known but tolerated or assumed away into irrelevance. It is almost heretical to approach things differently, at least from an academic perspective. Among financial market economists, who must deal with the world as it is, DSGE models are hardly used at all. The idea of a single general equilibrium that the economy will converge towards is nonsense, but the pulling power of this mythical state can easily override the dynamics that dominate over market-relevant horizons. Semi-structural models are simpler to estimate and use, yet they are typically more effective.

If the equilibrium state was realistic, we might be able to accept the short-term failings as being on route to a profitable place, but that isn't the case. All people and capital are not the same, or in the lingo, the factors of production are heterogeneous. These differences allow significant imbalances to accumulate. Some academics are attempting to incorporate heterogeneous agents in their models, but this typically involves grouping sectors, like households or companies. Doing so captures some imbalances but misses out the dynamics of how they correct. If there is one representative household with model-consistent expectations, they can't be responding to what other households are doing, or their expectations thereof. Because confidence is self-reinforcing between agents, confidence cycles are inherently nonlinear, and this influences the accumulation and unwinding of imbalances.

The existence of an imbalance does not mean it immediately exerts some slight pull to correct that is of any relevance. Momentum can potentially carry economies to massive imbalances before they become pertinent to the short term. In the interim, the economy is in a locally stable equilibrium. When the imbalances become a problem, that locally stable state ceases to be so, and an abrupt adjustment will need to occur towards the globally stable state. During the adjustment phase, resources will be underutilised, and a break relative to long-run trends happens. In the real world, there is not some neat steady state or unique equilibrium. What is stable is state dependent so an identical shock can have significantly different effects depending on the circumstances. That doesn't yield the nice consistent simulations many people want and expect, which helps discourage the use of what amounts to metastable equilibria. Nonetheless, metastability is more realistic and may eventually come to dominate the core of workhorse economic models in much the same way as it did in many other scientific fields.

Economies are big and slow, so observations of adverse dynamics are thankfully relatively rare. Financial markets experience such episodes far more frequently to varying degrees, so it is perhaps unsurprising that theoretical changes are better advanced here. No doubt it also helps that there is money motivating pragmatism and there are plenty of non-economists around to move things forward. The existence of multiple nonlinearities and sensitive dependence on initial conditions has to be embraced in real financial markets. Most asset returns are obviously not normally distributed, and the relationship between assets is similarly time-varying, with strong tail-dependence. Asset allocation models are evolving accordingly. While any overlaid views are informed by bad economic models, though, there will be periodic large misalignments in prices that will be exploitable by those with the right focus.

10.1.2 Misfocus

Most focus is typically given to flows, like employment growth, GDP, revenues or prices, which matter more to markets in normal times. Differences in view on these factors are tradable, as indeed are interest rates, both directly and for discounting future cash flows. Such changes tend to be quite small, but there are plenty of people who make a fine living chipping away with divergent views of this sort. The problem is that most market participants miss the wood for the trees by intensely monitoring the flows and ignoring the stocks that are accumulating. Stock imbalances are the fuel that drives the massive moves. Tracking the stocks and the potential triggers for correction can potentially flag the periodic trend changes that are highly profitable to ride. Monitoring potential catalysts for a correction should not be an afterthought here. A spark is needed to ignite the fuel of imbalance. Until a suitable spark occurs, imbalances can grow larger, and any counter-trend trades can sink underwater. Markets can be irrational in this sense for longer than most investors can remain solvent.

The wider the investment universe, the more often events will materialise that correct various imbalances. Most investors are constrained by the need to either stay near a benchmark or deliver stable positive returns, so bets on a trend changing are often inconsistent with the mandate. That leaves more room for those investors who do have flexibility. Even then, though, that doesn't mean it's a tradable strategy for many people. Direct engagement in the details of imbalances and potential triggers is time-consuming and will in the interim reveal other shorter-term trades. The temptation to trade for small gains here and there is natural, especially since such small deals can add up to significant sums. It is just important to keep the big payday trades in mind too, not least because when trends turn, some of those shorter-term trades can blow up far greater losses than the initially expected risk-reward.

Partly related to the excessively narrow focus on flows, CPI inflation has been central to demand management in recent decades. Mandates given to central banks are usually set relative to an inflation target, and the addition of GDP to the remit in some form does not dilute the problem much.

Central banks facing reasonably well-anchored inflation expectations tend to move policy in relation to the disinflationary margin of spare capacity in the economy, so there is already an indirect demand objective incorporated in an inflation target. The problem is that the horizon over which spare capacity is relevant and inflation controllable over means standard monetary policy instruments can not target wider imbalances. In the lead-up to the Great Recession, the policy was set to keep inflation down but not to lean against the huge credit boom. If policymakers had pushed back against the credit boom, the bubble wouldn't have grown as large, but inflation would have been too low relative to the target in contravention of the mandate. So, the nature of monetary policy targets meant there has tended to be an excessive focus on CPI inflation over classical monetary measures of inflation and credit.

When the financial sector is also stretched, stock imbalances can become far more dangerous. If banks don't have the capital to absorb losses, they may need to reduce assets, triggering a credit crunch in the process. And if there aren't enough liquid assets to sell, illiquid ones will need to be sold at an accordingly higher discount under such circumstances. When a fire sale depresses asset prices, marking to market trading books and repo margin requirements will trigger losses that can cause further sales. Financial market participants are tied together through their common assets where the problematic actions of one can cause others to do the same, which leads to inherently nonlinear price dynamics. Linkages can, of course, be direct too. Where one investor owns the liabilities of another, problems can spread quickly across the network. If leverage is low, such risk sharing can dilute shocks and aid stability, but high leverage can turn an idiosyncratic issue into a systemic one.

Neither financial balance sheets nor the network of liabilities historically had any following, and even now it is a fairly niche focus. Most economists disregard analysis of monetary data as quackery. Nonetheless, most regulators are now much more attuned to banking risks, and most financial sectors are in much better shape, including with fewer linkages between balance sheets in the financial network. However, that need not be true forever and certainly isn't true everywhere. Analysis along this dimension cannot be ignored, lest it contributes to an even larger correction. Either way, a problem in the real economy is a problem that can breed big trades, but when it comes to picking the best expression, knowing about banking sector problems, risk concentrations and network effects can help illuminate the best option. And the financial sector is also liable to provide the spark that causes other sectoral imbalances to correct, so it is often deserving of more focus from that angle as well.

10.2 Reshaping the Industry

Regulatory changes have done far more than just make banks more resilient. The macroprudential toolkit discussed in Chap. 6 is being deployed more often, with implications for the economy. It is also contributing to the wider incentive to shift risks to less regulated areas where profits can be more easily made. The next financial crisis will probably originate from one of these parts. That issue arises from the financial balance sheets, but there are individuals behind it who are drawn to the prospect of regaining personal upside, both financially and in time spent not crushed by bureaucracy. And as the structure of financial markets changes, so too do the demand for research. Expectations for market economists are evolving that are also influencing the supply, in many ways for the better.

10.2.1 Policies

The macroprudential policies discussed earlier addressed their use in a countercyclical setting—i.e. loosening when the credit cycle weakens and tightening when it advances. This cyclicality is prudent and should reduce the likelihood of banks being at the centre of the next financial crisis. Transitioning to the current state has involved significant increases in the required holdings of tier-1 capital and liquid assets, which has raised the cost of the balance sheet for banks. With less leverage, it is harder to generate returns that exceed a bank's cost of equity. Reduced profitability in a well-remunerated industry only leads to an orchestra of tiny violins playing, rather than an outcry, though. If this is the price of stability, most regulators will pay it gladly.

Additional balance sheet costs become problematic through the actual effect it has on bank behaviours. Staff are not just paid less. When the cost of holding assets increases, the profitability of the trading book diminishes and market makers can't sit on the risk the same way. Cocky refrains from brokers of "my size is your size" are tactfully replaced by talk of a partnership with investors seeking to execute large trades because banks can't comfortably take the other side of the trade anymore. When market conditions are healthy, with a steady two-way flow, this isn't necessarily a problem. If the broker knows the full size of the order to work, it can dip into incrementally execute the matching trade for the investor when the price is right. Some investors won't reveal their full-size up front, lest it moves the market, which can leave brokers angry when they've taken part of the risk themselves and seen successive order rounds shift prices against them. Fear of being run over like this only discourages them from making markets without immediate matchmaking of orders.

When an adverse shock hits the market, the loss of banks being able to trade as principal risk takers means that prices can gap far more dramatically before resistance is found. When few orders have been left in the market, large price changes are needed to awaken other investors to the value and step in. Some regulators hope that pension funds will take a long-term view and step in during such events to shore up the market, but those funds are typically far less active and more cautious than other investors. Buying during sharp price declines can feel as dangerous as catching a falling knife. Regular trading masks how bad market liquidity is nowadays. Quoted bid and ask prices on exchanges may be for such small volumes that they are unreflective of where the trade will take place. This gapping is masked in executed trade data by brokers finding a price to match trades and taking a small commission in the spread for the trouble. If liquidity isn't there when it is needed most, an adverse shock can cause an abrupt repricing of liquidity risk premia that compounds the price moves. A new source of procyclicality has been introduced via this regulatory route that is undesirable. Policymakers moaning about insufficient liquidity risk being priced in during bull markets are missing the root cause.

Reduced capacity for banks to warehouse risk is not just a function of increased balance sheet costs. Some regulators have taken some actions explicitly aimed at stopping banks from speculatively taking a risk on their own account. In the USA, proprietary trading has become heavily restricted within banks under Dodd-Frank. Meanwhile, in the UK, banks are being made to ring fence any retail operations from their other activities. The fear here is that speculative short-term trades might blow up and threaten the solvency of the whole institution, thereby potentially putting taxpayers at risk of bailing out the bank in the interests of the financial system's stability. Privatising profits when excessive losses are socialised is a controversial proposition.

Hard regulatory restrictions on bank structures are a solution to something that hasn't proved much of a problem. The credit boom before the Great Recession saw poor mortgage underwriting standards that ended in losses. That is the boring bread and butter business of a retail bank. Securitisation helped facilitate the credit growth, but losses stemmed from bad lending in the USA. Mortgage-backed securities in Europe were mostly fine. Neither prop trading restrictions nor ring fencing would have made much difference during the lead-up to the last financial crisis. Universal banking models diversify risk around the business in an efficient way. They are bigger beasts to bailout if there is a problem but the existence of banks structured like this does not meaningfully increase the probability of bailout. Arguably the opposite is true.

In other ways, regulators are fighting the last war with their stern focus on de-risking banks. That sometimes smells like a desire to punish, despite adverse side effects. For example, the EU's bonus cap encourages banks to raise fixed salaries instead, which reduces flexibility in compensation per worker and encourages turnover in headcount instead, and that is far costlier. Risks have a habit of concentrating in other areas as finance devises ways around regulatory restrictions. As much as regulators might think they're working with a precision machine, it is probably more akin to sausage making where regulation is the thin skin trying to constrain the financial sausage mix. Regulators who squeeze that skin too hard will risk a rupture that piles a mess uncontrollably elsewhere until a new skin can be slapped on it. In the current case, that risk is materialising in so-called shadow banks and central counterparties. Mandated use of the latter is simplifying the network of liabilities between banks, but it concentrates on inherently lightly capitalised clearers whose failure could close markets in a far more painful way than occurred during the credit crunch.

When the next financial crisis inevitably occurs, it is likely to originate from a shadow bank and be magnified through a clearer. Most Western banks are so well capitalised now that it would be difficult to bring a systemic one down. Stretched banking systems elsewhere are probably not sufficiently tied into the global system to cause a crisis, though, with the possible exception of China, where there would be significant trade effects too. As the memory of the last financial crisis fades and regulators change, other countries will probably row back some restrictions, and another banking crisis can develop, but that should be a long way off. Not having the same demands for bank bailouts in the next financial crisis is a high political priority. As the pressure is instead likely to emerge from relatively esoteric areas, like a clearing house, it should be more politically acceptable to deploy taxpayer funds in that direction. It is probably too cynical to think of politicians tweaking a trade-off of on where they'd rather bailout. The brutal reality is that most haven't got a clue about anything to do with finance.

10.2.2 People

Workers in the financial services industry don't have the luxury of being ignorant of how it works. Even if the pieces they have of the overall industry don't forewarn of structural changes elsewhere, they will feel the side effects of change. As it becomes more profitable to take risks on balance sheets outside of the banks, people naturally need to move to those institutions, and it similarly becomes more profitable for them to do so. Banks are unable to allow their traders to take the sort of risks that will enable them to make the returns anymore, so many of the best traders have been leaving for lightly regulated hedge funds. Other staff follow to perform the numerous support functions, but without as much compliance. That doesn't mean there's a shortage of demand for compliance and legal teams, though, as banks have been forced to increase their requirements massively. Nor does adding this headcount add to revenues. It probably subtracts from it and certainly adds to the cost base.

Even hedge funds have seen a rise in compliance requirements and maintaining greater flexibility to take risks does not mean that times are easy in this area of the market. Work is intense with lots of money on the line. With great risk can come great reward, but it can also blow up the fund and leave everyone looking for another job. There is also competition for extended bull markets. Hedge fund managers charge high fees with the promise of steady returns irrespective of the wider market performance. In downturns, this can provide end investors with an uncorrelated source of stability that is highly valued, but when markets are rising rapidly, the returns from many hedge funds can look weak in comparison. Fees have often been compressed relative to the old formula of two and twenty (i.e. 2% of assets under management and 20% of the upside).

Extremely loose monetary policy drove the extended bull market after the Great Recession, which creates this problem for hedge funds, even while aiding investors more generally. Passive fund managers offer the market return at minimal cost, and they have experienced an enormous increase in assets under management accordingly. This competition has posed more of a problem for conventional asset managers who aim to add value above the market benchmark but typically fail to do so consistently after taking the fees into account. Macro hedge funds have also had to adapt to the crushing of volatility by central banks, though, which makes it harder to find big themes that extend into large profits. There is something of a winner's curse for those who have done well too. High returns attract further assets under management, which makes it difficult to put on the sort of trades that did well before, and the reach into other areas can dilute the value of the best ideas for the fund. Some prominent fund managers have decided to downsize or even stop managing external funds for this reason.

Whether investors are taking a risk in a bank, hedge fund or another asset manager, there is still a need for research, but the requirements differ. Banks have tended to provide broad coverage in areas they actively trade in as an incentive for investors to deal with them. That model has been challenged on many fronts. Requirements for best execution mean that investors have to trade with the broker offering the best price rather than rewarding the bank providing the research underlying it. Monetising research has accordingly become more problematic, and with balance sheet also less profitable, many research teams have been hollowed out in an attempt to raise overall return on equity. European regulation (MIFID II) is also requiring banks to sell their research to investors at a price consistent with its cost, so bank research is adapting to a fundamental change. Many teams will not raise the revenue and be cut. Other teams will find star performers tire of subsidising their colleagues and leave to operate independently. Banks naturally need to support their risk takers too, but many may switch to using desk analysts who work directly for the traders and don't publish any research independent from that role.

Those banks switching to desk analyst models will become more like traditional investors who have long hired research teams to produce predominantly for internal consumption. The coverage area of each analyst is typically much wider, so they have to screen for opportunities and delve into those that are potentially most promising. Specialists in a field can provide invaluable assistance to that evaluation, but changes within the banks mean that there will be far fewer of them offering help of this sort. Independent research providers can pick up the slack, and this is likely to remain a rapidly growing area. Many of these companies are specialists in a particular country, asset class or sector, where reputation and connections are essential. Others provide a more generalist service aligned to be counterparts to their investing clients. A small group ar trying to replicate more comprehensive research offerings akin to what banks used to provide, and several will probably succeed.

Overall, the regulatory changes are likely to reduce the number of research analysts, even while far more will offer their product independently. This change could be hard for many specialists. For those not near the top of their field, it will be hard to find clients who will pay, especially as the choices become more transparent. Some specialists will become generalists while others will turn their hand to other lines of work. Those specialists who survive, or even thrive, will need to know their place in the market. Whether it is providing the best expert advice or screening towards that as a generalist, economists need to embrace the foibles of how real markets operate. Better mathematical capabilities would help with this as nonlinear dynamics, and potentially chaotic systems are modelled. With reduced headcount and uprated requirements to stand out, programming skills should also become more important. A bit of excel is woefully insufficient. Familiarity with specialist econometric software, like EViews, is also gradually being replaced by more powerful programming languages like python. To stand out, mastery of these more advanced technical skills will become increasingly important.

There will always be demand for rigorous analysis that respects real market economics. The framework from this book has built up the critical dimensions to consider, from the fundamental economic foundations, through the stabilising cross-beams, to the financial market coverage. And this final chapter has emphasised some significant gaps and how I see aspects of my industry evolving amid structural changes. As you deploy this framework and expand your knowledge along the dimensions that most interest you, I wish you the most profitable of adventures.

Further Reading

Arthur, Brian. 2015. *Complexity and the Economy*. Oxford University Press.

Strogatz, Steven. 2000. *NonlinearNonlinear Dynamics and Chaos: With Applications to Physics, Biology, Chemistry and Engineering*. Perseus Books.

Index

P. Rush, *Real Market Economics*,
https://doi.org/10.1057/978-1-349-95278-6

Printed by Printforce, the Netherlands